Gary Finley

9-3-68

CHURCH GROWTH IN JAMAICA

A PREVIEW OF THINGS TO COME IN MANY LANDS

BY

DONALD McGAVRAN

———

PRINTED AT THE LUCKNOW PUBLISHING HOUSE
LUCKNOW, U.P., INDIA.
1962

PREFACE

As Christian Mission takes church growth with renewed seriousness, it should recount meticulously how existing Churches have come into being and are now growing or stagnating. We should see the ways in which God has raised up Churches. What He has blessed in the past He is likely to bless in the future. We should also see ways in which (as Bishop Azariah used to say) "we frustrate God's work by our unbelief, indifference, or mismanagement of potential situations"; so that we can avoid offending Him.

These recountings will not be promotional devices to commend missions to supporters. These will be diagnostic writings setting forth what degree of church growth has been achieved, what mistakes have slowed advance, and what improvements are feasible. These will be written for Christians who, believing mission to be God's command, seek more effective ways of obediently multiplying churches.

Hundreds of statements are needed. In mission fields around the world are thousands of different populations, Churches with different degrees of vitality and ability to communicate, and missions with different biases, convictions, and denominational emphases. The Church grows differently in each population and needs accurate assessment. Church growth is a many-sided process. No one formula for it exists. The task is therefore to describe the precise Church which God has built in each specific population, and the ploughing, sowing, weeding, and reaping which have brought these particular sheaves into the Master's storehouse. Since each Church has its own individuality, founding mission, and heil geschichte this means hundreds of careful descriptions.

These writings on church growth should be done by many. To no one man has God granted a fraction of the insight needed to disclose the vast extent of His grace. Most men will know intimately only one population. Hence many writers of many different branches of the Church of Christ are needed. To avoid riding off in all directions at once, they should all bind themselves to a single task—describing the physical increase of the Church. The multiplication of sound Christian churches is obviously God's purpose. Nothing else will redeem the world or reconcile it to God. A church growth series is long over due.

These writings should be widely read; but this is impossible at present. What few studies exist were produced by one denomination in one land for its own immediate use. They have remained in manuscript or are out of print. Their message, limited to a few people, has now practically perished. The time has now come when all studies of church growth of whatever denomination (if done, not to commend it but to state what it has accomplished in finding and folding lost sheep) should be published and made widely available.

Men and women engaged in mission should read everything written on increasing the Church. None of it will be wholly applicable in other lands and Churches; but most of it will have a fair margin of value for those who take church extension seriously. Churches, Missions, and Boards could with profit spend considerable funds in research in church growth and publishing the results. Studies done by others, they should buy and distribute to their own nationals and missionaries. The most applicable researches should be translated.

"Church Growth in Jamaica" is offered in the hope that its realistic description may help Churches in Jamaica and every land obey the command in the first chapter of Genesis: "Be fruitful and multiply and fill the earth."

DONALD MCGAVRAN

1962   Institute of Church Growth

Northwest Christian College,

Eugene, Oregon, U.S.A.

TABLE OF CONTENTS

CHAPTER 1

JAMAICA—A PREVIEW OF THINGS TO COME IN MISSION

I. Jamaica Has Something to Say to Missions in Many Lands.

Starting about 1800 with a non-Christian population, it has become very largely "Christian". Many of the organizational adjustments, considered today as something new in missions, are an old story in Jamaica, where missions turned over to Churches[1] long ago, but still continue to assist them in many ways. One Jamaican Church became effectively self-governing in 1842. Others are almost as old. All are still assisted with missionaries and subsidies. Here we can see what has, in fact, happened when, to use today's phrases, "sovereign missions" became "assisting missions" and "paternalism" was replaced with "fraternalism."

Here a rather complete system of mission schools has operated under favorable circumstances for over a hundred years. In all the old-line Churches (Baptist, Methodist, Anglican, Presbyterian, Moravian, and Christian) parochial schools have created an educated elite who love the Christian Faith as their own. Church schools have educated practically all the leaders in government, education, commerce, and agriculture.

---

1. In this volume Church equals denomination, and church equals congregation.

True, Jamaica is different. No countries of Asia or Africa are like it. The present population of a million and a half rose out of four hundred thousand slaves freed in 1838. Having no ancient order to which it could cling, Jamaica has wholeheartedly accepted western civilization. The stable government is cordially linked to Britain. The language of the Island is English. Financially, Jamaica benefits by being part of the Caribbean playground of North America.

Despite these differences, Jamaica casts light on some important questions which world mission faces. For, in Jamaica, discipling is complete. No rival confronts the Christian Faith. The population as a whole is in the first stages of the perfecting process. The Churches of Jamaica face problems now, such as those in Congo, Thailand, and the Punjab will face when these lands too have been discipled. Thus Jamaica furnishes a preview of things to come in country after country around the world.

It is a preview in the devotion of its Christians. No one can visit the churches of Jamaica without being touched by the faithfulness of many members living radiant lives in the midst of widespread indifference, walking miles regularly to church, giving systematically, battling a sub-Christian social system, and voicing wonderful prayers full of tender meaning.

It is a preview in its demonstration of brotherhood. The churches are full of Christians of every color, worshipping side by side. Bright eyed children—white, coffee, mahogany, and ebony colored—pour out of church schools, hands full of books, laughing and talking as they go home.

It is a preview in the emancipation and elevation wrought by Christ. The creation of the Christian upper

classes—genuinely Jamaican and genuinely cultured—out
of the raw materials here in 1838 has been a huge task in
which the Churches have played a major part. The educational system, the wonderful roads, the burgeoning city
of Kingston, courage in the face of earthquakes and hurricanes, the heroism of William Knibb the British missionary
and George William Gordon the Jamaican Baptist patriot,
the cultivation of steep hillsides, the upsurge typified
by the change from wattle walls and thatch roofs in
1920 to the solid walls and zinc sheeted roofs of today,
the beautiful English of the classes, and the University
College recently established,—all bespeak efforts of government, commerce, and Jamaican leaders stimulated, aided
and rectified by the Christian Faith. The Church throughout the world will probably not create new civilizations
all by itself. But, as in Jamaica, it will add that irreplace-
able guidance of God without which the ablest of men and
nations end their wilderness wanderings in Gomorrah not
Jerusalem.

Jamaica is also a preview in that it stands at the dawn
of a new day. It has untapped resources, a wealth of man
power, and wonderful twelve month a year climate. Its
young men are seeing visions of a population freed from
race pride which, as in many lands, has shackled vast numbers. Christian national leaders dream of a state where
every citizen is educated, a disciple of Christ, and a pro-
ducer of the common wealth. Better, they are working to
bring these dreams to pass. The new nation is feeling its
wings, eradicating old ills, and striving to make this island
a paradise on earth, with a stabilized population, Christian
hillsides, towns, and cities, and a social order marked with
equal opportunity, justice, and freedom for all. Indeed,

this is God's will for it. Elsewhere too as Christ redeems more and more persons this sense of working together with "the God and Father of our Lord Jesus Christ" will, in land after land, render more effective the many strivings toward progress.

Jamaica is a preview in its problems as well as in its hopes. How does western cultural overhang handicap the extension of the churches? Should Gathered Churches build themselves from un-shepherded persons 'belonging' to other Churches? Can one congregation serve the classes and the masses, or should congregations be formed according to the economic and educational status of the members? What should the Church say about the sex standards of the masses? How can a younger Church use missionaries of another land when their pay, inexperience, foreign training, and out-of-touchness with the common man interpose so many barriers to effectiveness? And how can mission boards, receiving Macedonian calls from many lands, continue resources to younger Churches which seem content to remain static, run the machinery, and receive perpetual subsidies from abroad?

These and many other world-wide problems present themselves in Jamaica. This study will not speak specifically to each one. It will illumine some more than others. Churchmen from various countries may differ in their estimates of the degree to which Jamaican church development resembles that of their own lands; but we hope they will find a fair margin of value here. No situation is ever exactly like another and true parallels are rare. Yet the Christianization of any land furnishes some lessons to younger Churches in other lands and their assisting missions. Any notable discipling—and such is Jamaica's—is

highly instructive to all who take the Great Commission
seriously.

II. **This Volume Discusses the Growth of the Churches in Jamaica**

What has really happened? What objective results
have occurred in the discipling of Jamaica? What church
growth has taken place? Only a true description of
Jamaican phenomena will serve a useful purpose. Vague
idealistic statements of aims will not do. This volume
will help assess mission in Jamaica and cast light on
mission elsewhere, only if it is exact and faithful to the
facts. Understanding is the primary need.

To understand church growth, it must be seen in relation to the history, culture, education, classes, and masses
of the land where it is going on. No one can describe the
churches correctly except he know at least something
of the sociology, psychology, land tenure, and aspirations
of a land. Wide reading on Jamaica, living there for some
time, and discussing this manuscript with Jamaican friends
have added to my understanding of the ground in which the
churches have multiplied. But "ground" is a vast field.
No man can hope to depict it in exact proportions.
Indeed, what are the true proportions depends on what
is the true perspective—and there are many different
opinions.

In presenting the background, my bias, which I
cheerfully confess, is that I see Jamaica not primarily in
contrast to England or America, but rather in comparision
with the Philippines, India, Africa, Thailand, and other
lands where my residence and studies of church growth
have necessitated understanding the structure of society

and the Churches. I see the Jamaican Churches in comparison with other younger Churches. I see the island manifesting many characteristics of other tropical lands. In its development it has met some different and many of the same circumstances. It is now more advanced than most of its sister countries and has much to say to world mission everywhere.

The broad picture presented of the Churches and of society (Chapters II, III, IV and V) is reasonably accurate. Membership figures for each denomination across the century have been taken from governmental sources and checked against church publications. The population figures and charts are from current publications of the Vital Statistics Officer of the West Indian Federation.

Chapter VI depicting one denomination—The Christian Church—furnishes detail essential to understanding how churches grow in Jamaica. Church growth —a most complex process—must always be studied in particular situations. The Church always grows in the concrete, never in the abstract. Churches are made up of particular individuals in particular strata of population. Church growth cannot be understood "in general" or in accordance with theological doctrines operating in a vacuum. Chapter VI anchors church growth to bread fruit and ackee eating Jamaicans on these fertile hillsides. As we see this one specific Church growing and not growing in its own neighbourhoods, out of its own ecclesiastical and theological history, we shall understand the discipling, multiplying process better. Other Churches in Jamaica will have slightly different growth patterns; but all of them will be more like the one recounted in chapter six than like English, African, or American patterns.

The chapter has been checked with the ministers of the Christian Church, and is an exact account of what church growth has been in this particular galaxy of congregations. Here are recorded the significant facts concerning their birth, development, characteristics, weaknesses and strengths. Here is stated what is necessary to get this stalled younger Church going again. This is the way these congregations look to an impartial friend, whose business is examining Churches to discern their structure, growth patterns, and opportunities to expand.

We hope this frank description will be of value to churchmen around the world. While Jamaican ways and Christian Church ways are not exactly their ways, they will find much that bears on their problems and, perhaps, even illuminates them.

We trust that it will also help missionary minded men and women in the churches of England and America see what their missions face. Mission is not merely a wonderful and mysterious process. The propagation of the Faith can be seen and understood in terms of the sociology, history, economic and racial ground in which it is going on. We trust this book will promote real understanding of how younger Churches grow and—on occasion—do not grow. World mission has everything to gain and nothing to lose by an accurate view of the process.

CHAPTER II

HOW HAS THE CHURCH GROWN IN JAMAICA?

Growth of the churches takes place by increase of members. As countable men and women become disciples of Christ, churches grow in size and multiply in numbers.

It is true that uncountable qualitative growth—in goodness, humility, patience, obedience, and love—is vitally important to the Church; and also that under some circumstances quantitative increase may result in a very thin embodiment of the mind of Christ. It is equally true that Christianity, to disciple the nations and to please God, must multiply enormously. For example, it was the multiplying multitudes of surrendered Christians of the Methodist revival which made it of such great significance in the history of the world. Had Wesley's disciples remained only a few dozen in number they would have played a very small part in God's labors of redemption. It is impossible to Christianize a country by reconciling only one per cent of its people to God—no matter how thoroughly reconciled they may be! Nations cannot be Christianized without significant growth in the number of Christians.

As long as two men can lift more than one, numbers are important. Numbers of the saved are never "mere". No mother, rejoicing in one child saved from a burning building, could forget the other ten who had not been rescued, comforting herself with the "spiritual" thought that numbers are not important. Reconciling nations to God involves reconciling very considerable numbers of men to God. Indeed, remembering that our Lord came to save sinners, one must presume that the more sinners saved the better pleased He is. In Luke's parable of the great banquet, the king is urgent that his hall be filled. Ontologically speaking, the structure of the universe and the nature of God are such that since the redemption of the entire creation is the ultimate goal, salvation has both quantitative and qualitative dimensions.

We stress this point because a rationalization of defeat has gained wide credence in the last few decades. It has been popular to decry numbers of Christians. We doubt if this is sound th nking. On the contrary, it seems reasonable to believe that if a hundred thousand Christians are good, two hundred thousand are better. They can cast twice as many votes for just wages, give twice as much to the poor, and proclaim the Good News to twice as many sinners. They are a step in the direction of that day when "every knee" shall bow and "every tongue" confess.

Hence in this study we take quantitative growth seriously. We seek the facts of physical growth. We want to see how in Jamaica disciples of the Lord Jesus increased from perhaps one per cent of the population in 1800 to their present proportion. We shall graphically depict this process, noting how the different denominations grew, what part of the population has become Christian, and what part yet remains out of the Church.

I. The First Stage of Christianization.

In the eighteenth century Jamaica was one of England's richest colonies, producing fabulous amounts of sugar. Slaves were imported from Africa to work the plantations. Only they could stand the malarious climate. English owners, attracted by enormous profits, came out in small numbers, built great houses,—and died at the average age of thirty. In 1838 an accurate census showed 400,000 slaves. It is likely that their numbers had stood at about this figure for a number of decades.

Till about 1790, despite a few slave baptisms in the Anglican and Presbyterian churches of the plantation owners, the slaves by and large had no opportunity to know the Gospel. They were solidly animist. Then Methodist missionaries arrived and began to establish churches, chiefly among the mulattos and quadroons in the towns and villages. These men and women, in whom flowed the blood of both Africa and England, had often had privileges of association and education denied to the full blooded African. They formed a different "caste". Some had been freed. Some owned property. Some had been educated. Some served as foremen. They felt a distaste for the animism of the black slaves. Yet they were not welcome in the plantation owners' churches. They were, unknowingly, longing for the Gospel. The Methodists found this stratum of population highly responsive. Methodist churches were founded rapidly throughout it. Soon practically the entire stratum had become Methodists.

About 1790 a few Tories in the United States, finding the democratic government little to their liking, emigrated to Jamaica with their slaves—who in the United States had become Baptists. Their slaves started establishing Baptist churches among the other slaves in a perfectly natural extension of their own joyful Christian faith. This was frowned upon by the plantation owners. Chapels were burned and the spread of "Baptist sects" among the slaves was severely penalized.

About 1800 British Baptists started sending missionaries to Jamaica. These Englishmen were accustomed to opposition to their non-conformity, and were men of deep personal faith. They soon became champions of the slaves and began using Christian slaves as local pastors. Within thirty years, 20,000 slaves in the face of considerable persecution had become communicant members in the missionary Baptist churches. Others were members of the spontaneous Baptist churches which grew up here and there. It is not too much to say that the pure Africans went largely Baptist while "the coloreds" went largely Methodist. Moravians, Congregationalists, Presbyterians, and finally Anglicans also did missionary work among the slaves and planted churches.

Time will not permit more than this brief summary of the early days. In 1838 the slaves were freed. We pass over the intervening dozen years and pick up the story in 1850.

In the middle of the nineteenth century, missions can be said to have completed the first phase of their labors. Churches had been established throughout the island. The animism of Africa could never again become the religion of the common people—though animistic practices and bush medicine persisted down through the years. Fifteen per cent of the population were communicant members in some church, which means that about thirty per cent of the total population were consciously Christian. About one in every three persons on the island was either a communicant or a child in the family of communicants.

II. The Present Situation in Regard to Population and Church Membership.

In the 1951 census, the population of Jamaica is given as 1,400,000. Jamaica like other lands is in the midst of a population explosion. George W. Roberts, Vital Statistics Officer of the Federation of the West Indies, in his authoritative book, *The Population of Jamaica*, projects a probable population in 1958 of 1,670,000, in 1961 of 1,800,000, and in 1971 of 2,250,000. These are the numbers with which Christian mission today is concerned: The Churches in Jamaica and their assisting missions have as their God-given task making disciples of eighteen hundred thousand in 1961 and twenty two hundred thousand ten years later.

How many of these multitudes are Christians now? The latest information places the communicant membership of the main Churches of Jamaica as follows.

Old-Line Churches		Other Evangelical Churches	
Jamaica Union Baptist Church	... 26.000	Assemblies of God and Churches of God	... 40,000
Christian Church	... 4.000	Brethren and Holiness	... 10,000
Church of England	... 44,000	S.D. Adventist Church	... 27.000
Congregational Church	... 3,000	Churches of Christ	... 7.000
Methodist Church	... 21,000	Other Baptists	... 10,000
Moravian Church	... 6,000		
Presbyterian Church	... 12,000		
Total	116,000	Total	94,000

Roman Catholics claim 100,000, which may mean 15,000 communicants, though we assume it means 30,000.

The figures in the first column are not debated. However, it must be remembered that in all communicant lists there is likely to be error—non-residents, the cold and indifferent, those who are leading unbecoming lives, and even some who are dead. The other Churches often say that the "Anglican 44,000" would be much smaller if membership in the Anglican Church meant what it does in the Methodist or Baptist Churches.

The figures in the second column are vigorously debated. Yet they are what these Churches themselves claim. When I see little and big Churches of God on every hillside and in every town throughout Jamaica and in every section of Kingston-St. Andrews, I hesitate to disbelieve the 40,000. When I see the membership figure of 27,000 for the Adventist Church backed up by a per capita giving of 17 pounds per member per year into the central treasury at Mandeville, I cannot question its accuracy. The "Other Baptist" figures were given me by eminent Jamaica Baptist Union ministers. The figures for the Brethren were given by responsible leaders in their Church.

It is noticeable that none of the Churches in the first column are growing and that all those in the second column are. The Roman Catholics also, regarding Jamaica as a ripe mission field, are pouring in American priests and money and growing at a great pace.

Some interesting proportions may be noted.

Taking the population of the Island at 1,600,000 in 1956 and the communicant membership listed above as a fair approximation for that year, and remembering that of the 1,600,000, 1,024,000 persons are adults (15 years of age and above), we may make the following statements.

Comparing communicants with total adults, we may say that:—

1 out of 9 is a communicant in the old-line Churches,

1 out of 11 is a communicant in other evangelical Churches,

1 out of 34 is a communicant in the Church of Rome,

1 out of 4 is a communicant in all Churches put together.

Comparing "Christian community"[1] with total population, we may say that:—

1 in 7 belongs to the community of the old-line Churches,

1 in 8 belongs to the community of other evangelical Churches,

1 in 27 belongs to the community of the Roman Catholic Church,

1 in 3 belongs to the general "Christian" community.

Remembering that a large per cent of the classes are communicants but only a small per cent of the masses, we hazard a further estimation as follows. The exact truth based on careful research might be even more startling.

Of the 1,024,000 adults, about 100,000 belong to the classes and about 900,000 to the masses, In the old-line Churches (membership 116,000) at least half of the members or about 60,000 are of the classes. This leaves about 60,000 communicants from among the 900,000 adults of the masses. Thus *only one out of 15 of the adults of the masses* is a member in the old-line Churches.

The other evangelical Churches have probably 90 per cent of their members from the masses. Thus out of their 94,000 communicants, probably 85,000 come from

---

(1) In estimating "Christian community" the fairest procedure is to disregard denominational claims, and simply multiply communicants (usually a responsible figure) by 2, assuming that we shall thus get those children who are, in fact, being reared by practicing Christians and really belong to the Christian community.

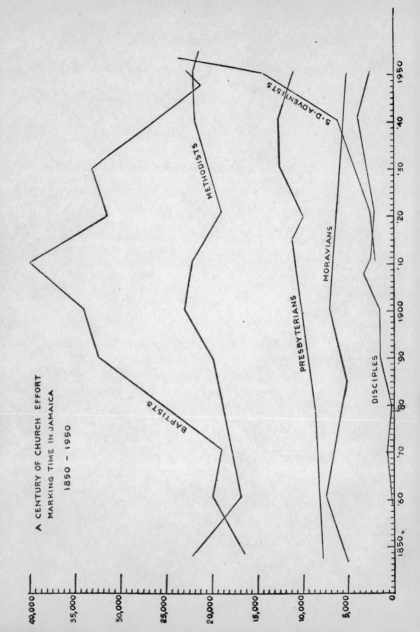

A CENTURY OF CHURCH EFFORT
MARKING TIME IN JAMAICA
1850 – 1950

BAPTISTS

METHODISTS

PRESBYTERIANS

MORAVIANS

S.D. ADVENTISTS

DISCIPLES

40,000
35,000
30,000
25,000
20,000
15,000
10,000
5,000
0

1850   '60   '70   '80   '90   1900   '10   '20   '30   '40   1950

the masses. This means that about *one in nine of the adults of the masses are communicants in other evangelical Churches.*

Summarizing these findings negatively for the old-line Churches we may say that:—

8 out of 9 adults in the Island are not their communicants,

14 out of 15 adults of the masses are not their communicants, and

6 out of 7 of the total population are not in their communities.

III. Marking Time for a Century in Jamaica.

On the accompanying graph, we have plotted the growth of the five non-conformist[1] Churches present during the century 1850 to 1950. Each line depicts one Church and shows the number of its members decade by decade. Let the eye follow each line in turn

During this century each Jamaica Church was assisted by a mission, usually from England though one of them was from America. Bands of missionaries from four to forty strong, worked with their Jamaican churches, pastoring, preaching, administering, running schools, and teaching in seminaries.

The fact which leaps out at us from this graph is that despite the favorable circumstances—no hostile government, no rival religion, no civil disturbances or revolutions,

---

1. We omit the Anglican figures from this graph for two reasons: (1) The significant growth of the Anglican Church was due largely to its privileged position as the *established* Church. Since establishment does not now, nor will it in the future influence church growth in many lands, it is confusing to bring it in here. (2) The first five Churches shown did not grow—whatever others might have done. When considered alone they raise pertinently the question "Is mission aid in perpetuity to stopped Churches?"

the continual service of considerable numbers of missionaries, and over the hundred years the additional strength
of millions of pounds and dollars—practically no church
growth occurred.   Each line runs along at about its own
level.   It has some ups and downs, makes a small gain,
and comes out about where it went in.   Methodists started
with 21,000 and came out a hundred years later with
21,000. Moravians started the century with 5,500 and
ended it with 5000.

We have not been able to discover the cause of the
great growth and decline of the Jamaica Union Baptist
Church.   It became an independent Church in 1842, a
hundred years before devolution became popular in most
mission fields.   Some say that other believers' baptism
Churches have grown largely at Baptist expense.   Others
say the liberal-fundamentalist controversy split off thousands. However that may be, the Jamaica Union Baptists,
too, end the century close to where they began it.

To put the matter in a nutshell, when the 1950
figures are compared with the 1850, all the old line denominations are seen to have been marking time as far as
discipling is concerned, while receiving continuous,
century-long mission aid.

During this century they concentrated on perfecting.
They built churches—and rebuilt them after earthquakes
and hurricanes.   They gathered pupils, trained teachers,
made primary education widely available, and secondary
available to all who could pay for it. In the local churches
they worshipped God and reared generation after generation of Christians.   These, in their men's and women's
organizations, Sunday Schools and Christian Endeavors,
prayer meetings and building committees, practiced the

Christian religion and grew in grace. Out of all this, the denominations developed an educated Christian upper class and induced in the masses a respect for the Church and a vague allegiance to it. Most babies, for example, are baptized or dedicated in the church even if the parents never worship there.

While this was going on, church members did not increase. The Churches were perfecting those already in and lifting them to middle class status. Jamaica furnishes a fine illustration of imbalance between discipling and perfecting. Very large numbers remained unchurched. The Church was either unable to bring them to Christian commitment or content not to do so.

Was the Church *unable* to bring them to Christian commitment? In later chapters we shall observe a very large block of the population which appeared inaccessible to the Churches. We shall understand how they failed to make much impression on it.

Was the Church *content* not to do so? When a Church meets a great obstacle, it adjusts to it and learns to live with it. In regard to the huge numbers of unchurched men and women in Jamaica, the Church became content with, or at least resigned to, their living outside the Church.

Since the Church in all lands meets inaccessible blocks of population, world mission should observe the way in which the old-line Jamaican Churches (1) developed forms and characteristics which insulated them still further from the unchurched masses, (2) interpreted their task almost exclusively in terms of perfecting, and (3) played down discipling as a regrettable emphasis on numbers involving an indefensible lowering of the standards.

The above paragraphs take on additional meaning when we ask whether the unchurched were really inaccessible? Were the old-line Churches really shut up to no growth? The Seventh Day Adventist line cuts all these static Churches like a knife. Our first impulse is to scorn such growth as something our churches should not seek. But first impulses are seldom good. Erroneous as we believe the Adventist doctrines to be at the point where they equate the Old Testament and the New and forget that our Lord is the fulfilment of the inner intent of the Law, we admire their consecrated Christian lives, their admirable biblical stewardship, their independent self-respect, and their business-like conduct of the affairs of the Church. We wonder whether we cannot learn as much from them today as the Jamaica Anglicans have from what in 1815 they called "the dark and dangerous fanaticism of the Methodists"!

With both the Church of Rome and the Church of the Adventists making great numerical gains in Jamaica, scornfully dismissing concern about church growth as a "superficial desire for quick results" seems neither necessary nor sensible. Granting that the Church must be a company of the redeemed, a Household of God, manifesting the life of Christ both as regards individual holiness and as regards society, and becoming increasingly relevant to modern man and modern society, the old-line Churches should realize that unless they win a much larger proportion of the population in Jamaica they will be able neither to influence the direction society takes, nor to speak cogently to the twentieth century. They will be even more handicapped in the twenty-first, after the explosion of population has continued for some time!

If, in the midst of winnable masses in this fair isle, the five old-line Churches shown in the graph somehow or other manage to be satisfied with about 60,000 communicants, they might ponder the depth of their own discipleship If they cannot redeem the masses, they can scarcely claim a vital connection with the *Saviour*. He died that Jamaicans might be saved. Any Branch of His Church which finds itself powerless to bring the masses into redemptive relationship to our Lord may very well question its connection with Him — Who came to save publicans and sinners and went to the cross to do it. Scorn for mere numbers would seem to be neither Christian — nor perhaps prudent — in Jamaica today.

At this precise point Jamaica has much to say to world mission. The graphs of many younger Churches look startlingly like these of Jamaica. The causes of arrested growth are different in each church. Few of them stop for Jamaican reasons. But they stop. The comfortable idea that the younger Churches once established will grow of themselves is a myth, perhaps even a rationalization. We deceive ourselves when we think that the trouble can be rectified by organizational adjustments—merging various small younger Churches, turning from "paternalism to fraternalism," or transforming sovereign missions into assisting missions. These may on occasion be expedient moves but by themselves they will not get stalled younger Churches going again. They do not necessarily advance the central continuing business of mission.

IV. **The Widening Gap**

This truth is emphasized, when we ponder the declining percentage of communicants, shown on the acompanying graph.

In 1850 the population of Jamaica was 400,000 and the communicant membership was about 60,000 — including, of course, the Anglicans whose growth figures have not been plotted in the preceding graph. Thus the communicants in 1850 were about 15 per cent of the total population. A hundred years later in 1950 the population was 1,400,000 and the communicants of the same old-line Churches numbered 116,000 which was 8 per cent of the total. While the absolute number had increased, the proportions had declined from 15 per cent to 8 per cent. The number of non-communicants had jumped from 360,000 to about 1,200,000.[1]

As to the future, if Mr. Robert's projection is correct and if the Churches remain generally static making only a slight increase, then the old-line communicants will decline to 7 per cent of the population in 1961 and to 6 per cent in 1971.

We can get at the same basic fact in another way. Let us ask (1) how much must the old-line Churches grow in the 15 years, 1956 to 1971, to remain 8 per cent of the population; and (2) how much must they grow to climb to the 15 per cent position they held a century ago in 1850? The answers are: (1) to remain 8 per cent of the population they must grow from 116,000 communicants to 180,000. This is slight growth and would involve for these 15 years

----

1. The gap for the Baptists, Methodists, Presbyterians and Moravians considered by themselves is much more striking. In 1850 their communicants made up about 13% of the population. In 1950 they comprised 4%. In 1850 non-communicants of these four Churches numbered 350,000, in 1950 1,345,000.

When Churches cease to grow, this is what happens. When they look out on the unsaved multitudes with equanimity, they consign themselves to a diminishing role. God sends others to search for the lost. And if these others disobey God, Satan sends in his servants.

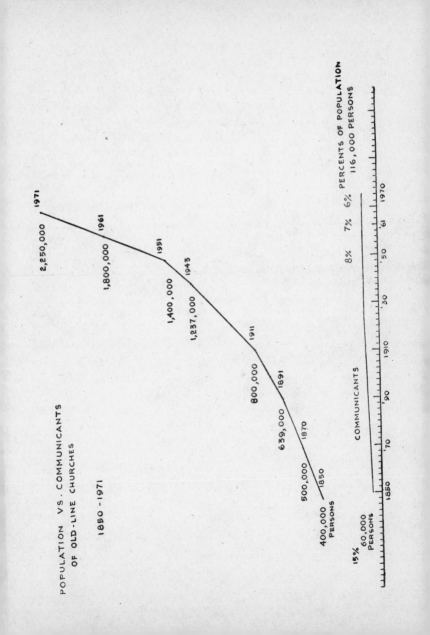

POPULATION VS. COMMUNICANTS
OF OLD-LINE CHURCHES

1850 - 1971

2,250,000 1971
1,800,000 1961
1951
1,400,000 1943
1,237,000
1911
800,000 1891
639,000 1870
500,000 1850
400,000 PERSONS

PERCENTS OF POPULATION
8%   7%   6%   116,000 PERSONS

COMMUNICANTS

'50   '61   1970
1930   1910   '90   '70   1850

15% 60,000 PERSONS

a net annual gain of only 4,500 or 5 per cent. (2) To regain the 15 per cent position, however, they would have to increase to 337,000 communicants, a gain of 221,000. Achieving this would require for each of the 165 years a net yearly increase of 15,000 for 13 per cent. Such a gain would not be easy, but for resolute men empowered by the Holy Spirit, it should be quite possible. If there be any spiritual descendants of Henry Morgan, William Knibbs or George William Gordon in Jamaica, it can be done. God, we assume, actively desires it.

As we ponder these static younger Churches, we are at the heart of one of the main questions facing world mission. Why are so many younger Churches bogged down? Since missionary assistance to younger Churches involves collossal sums of money and the lives of considerable numbers of fraternal delegates, what is the correct policy toward younger Churches like these in Jamaica?

These questions in turn depend on others. Is the situation that in Jamaica younger Churches *cannot* grow? Is the 75 per cent of the population now out of any church really unreachable? If so, then how do we account for the growth of the Churches of God? And the Church of Rome?

Before we answer these questions, let us look carefully at two characteristics of Jamaican society. Both have a close bearing on the variety, quality, and amount of church growth.

CHAPTER III

THE CLASSES AND THE MASSES

Church growth in Jamaica is conditioned to a unique degree by the class-mass structure of society. Before anyone can understand how churches grow here, he must discern the basic forms of this society. He must realize that Jamaica is a country of clearly defined classes and masses separated by a deep wide gulf.

Such social structure is strange to the western mind. It is contrary to both democratic and Christian theory. It is known in neither England nor America where a shallow valley between the upper and lower classes is bridged by large middle classes.

In Jamaica also there are 'middle classes', but they are so small and, compared to the masses, so well off, that it is misleading to direct attention to them. A truer picture is obtained if it is noted that they and the upper classes together form the top few per cent of the population.

Society made up of two to ten per cent classes and ninety to ninety eight per cent masses may be strange to the western mind, but it is common in many countries of the world. This is in part what makes Jamaica important to world missions. Most younger Churches operate in the Jamaican kind of social order. They seek to disciple not equalitarian populations, but those where the vast majority lives on a subsistence basis while a tiny minority lives a relatively rich life.

Shall the Church propagate itself among the classes or the masses? Can it grow among both? Shall ministers belong to the classes or the masses? And be recompensed according to what standard? Can churches of the masses hold their educated youth or will it migrate up into the churches of the classes? How can we create a ministry which can win the masses, keep them really Christian, and derive its living from them? How can a Church keep from having large numbers of illiterate, inarticulate and nominal 'Christians' in its membership,—without becoming an exclusive upper class institution? In the day of the common man, how can a small Church of the classes adapt quickly enough to survive? How can a Church of the classes father a kind of congregation which will multiply indefinitely among the masses? And thus make available to them the power of God to salvation which they so greatly need to liberate from the oppressor within. These practical questions are asked in many countries. Jamaica is a laboratory in which world mission sees one set of answers which have been actually given.

The rest of this chapter will be spent in describing what class-mass society looks like in Jamaica. The description may startle the reader, for visitors to Jamaica usually spend time with the cultured of the Island—the classes. Visitors rarely sense the magnitude or condition of the masses, to say nothing of what they mean for church growth.

I. The Social Structure of Jamaica

The distinction between the tiny classes and the huge masses here is not that known in Michigan or Manchester between the rich and the poor. It is more like the distinction in Mississippi between the Whites and the Negroes, though the difference in Jamaica does not rest on color.

Jamaica is somewhat like India with its upper and lower castes. The Brahmans are mostly light colored—though a few are dark; and the Shudras are mostly dark colored—though a few are light. Hinduism sanctified and legalized the color distinction and made it into the caste system. It is impossible to climb from one caste to another and immoral to try to do so. Climbing is not impossible or immoral in Jamaica, but it is difficult. Christianity and West Indian law theoretically hold open the door to equality of opportunity; but inherited wealth in the hands of the classes, a high school and college system which makes education available chiefly to those able to pay for it, the universal tendency of the "haves" to guard their privileges, and the small social conscience among educated Christians, all combine to make exit from the masses difficult.

In the few cases where exit is achieved, it becomes a two generation process. In the first generation, an able man of the masses, through hard work and good furtune, working abroad for a dozen years, or in some other way builds up ten to twenty acres of land, a little store, a garage or cycle repair shop, and sends his son or daughter (often with mission help), to high school, through "the Jamaica locals" to teacher training, ministerial training or other outlet. The young person, if successful, finds himself in the lower ranks of the classes. He must amass wealth and buy property before his position is really secure.

Merle Davis, the distinguished sociologist and churchman who studied the Church in Jamaica in 1942, wrote that society consists of—(1) "a small class of planters and estate owners......Here is good breeding, a sense of noblesse oblige, a familiarity and friendliness, together with disillusionment with the Jamaican working classes who are descended from former slaves......(2) a group of educated Jamaicans with both European and African blood in their veins. Many are graduates of colleges and English universities......They are the barristers, doctors, teachers, pastors, and government officials. They are the leaders of the masses of uneducated and under privileged, and yet they are *vastly far* above them...... (3) *Far below* this group and constituting an *altogether different* world is the Jamaican proletariat—the hewers of wood and drawers of water—who provide the bulk of labor and constitute the numerous, shifting, unattached class of workers. Ninety per cent of the island population are class three and live in scattered villages, hamlets, and homesteads, and in barracks or cottages on large estates ......Outwardly conforming to the sanctions of the Western European way of life, the bulk of the people are still swayed by other than these sanctions." The words underlined by me indicate that Dr. Davis saw clearly this deep wide gulf between the classes and the masses.

Smith and Kruijer, sociologists, writing in 1957 a "Manual for Extension Workers in the Caribbean" for the Government, say concerning the land holders among the masses, i.e. the upper section of the masses, "For the majority of our small holders, the legal processes relating to land are too expensive, unfamiliar, and unpredictable. Small holders therefore try to arrange their land dealings among themselves with as little recourse to the law courts as possible. There are thus two systems of tenure,—that which conforms to legal procedures, and that of a customary and extra-legal nature." Thus at the base of society —land tenure—even the upper strata of the masses find

the law of the land to be Saul's Armour and arrange their
land transactions by word of mouth. A "Facilities for
Titles" law, recently passed, will alleviate this condition;
but that it was necessary testifies to the existence of the
masses.

Smith and Kruijer also speak to the economic gap
between the classes and the masses. "The most wealthy
people, large produce dealers, merchants, and large land
owners form the town's elite. Other upper class people are
physicians, solicitors, teachers, ministers, and highly placed
government officials. These are only very rarely found
living in the rural areas away from towns."

"At the top of the social hierarchy in the villages and
open country are the ministers of religion, teachers, nurses,
post mistresses, sergeants of police, government officials,
and perhaps some better off shopkeepers and farmers. The
lower classes in these areas consist mainly of farmers and
laborers, but the differences in status among these are so
marked that the lower classes have often been said to be
five: (1) The 'bigger men' or 'big shots' (often addressed as
Mass) who never hire themselves out, who do not work
day-for-day, who employ laborers more or less regularly,
and who make a relatively decent living. (2) Independents
who own enough land so that they never hire themselves
out, but not enough to employ others. (3) Cultivators,
who own a few acres, but do hire themselves out on occasion. (4) Laborers who do not own land. (5) Beggars,
invalids, and others who cannot work. The three lowest
sub-classes constitute the majority......Two thirds of all
males in classes 1, 2 and 3, are in class 3." And, it might
be added, nearly ninety per cent of the masses are in
classes, 3, 4, and 5.

"The classes own cars: the masses walk or ride bicycles or buses" is largely true. There are, however, some whose education places them in the classes, without enough money for a car; and there are a few successful men of the masses who buy cars—when their business requires it.

The classes form less than 10 per cent of the population. The masses form more than 90 per cent. The economic gap is vividly seen in the fact that the income of the upper bracket clerks, teachers, ministers, small business men, government servants, runs $1500—$3000 a year; while that of the laborer, renter, small cultivator and independent runs $200—$300 a year. The really poor have still less.

There is a huge educational gap between the classes and the masses. The masses have many illiterates, many who have only two to four years schooling, and a relative few who have had six to eight years. The classes are educated people, read newspapers, magazines, and books, and are cultured citizens of the world. They have passed Senior Cambridge Examinations or the equivalent and graduated from colleges and universities.

In 1953 there were only 8,000 students in high school in Jamaica out of a population of 1,400,000. Roughly one in two hundred got a chance (at his parents' expense) to obtain high school education—the Key to the Classes. Government proposes to increase the number of high school students. Twelve thousand are now in high school and government would like to have twenty-six thousand. Eighteen hundred freeships (scholarships which pay tuition and in some cases board) are now awarded annually by government to those who pass with high enough marks a competitive examination at the end of the Elementary School.

This is a good move, but the children of the classes have an enormous advantage in any competitive examination. When a boy, who has grown up speaking beautiful English, in a home blessed with books, economic security, cameras, cars, special tutoring, and great concern for education, competes with a boy from a typical home of the masses, there is no question who will win. Most scholarships go to sons and daughters of teachers, merchants, policemen, 'big shots' and ministers. Not many go to sons of the landless or of one acre peasants.

There has also been a clear cut racial gap in Jamaica. The classes were composed of those who had European and African blood in their veins; the more European blood and the lighter the color, the higher the standing. The masses were made up of dark skinned people. The myth that light color goes with ability, dependability, and industry, reinforced this racial gap, The fact that ability is equally shared by men of all colors and races is beginning to bridge the gap. Some leaders of Jamaica are dark skinned. In all churches, schools, and business one finds people of all colors. There is no color bar in Jamaica. There is effective brotherhood.

Yet the racial gap lingers on. One continually hears that the dark skinned find it hard to succeed. As between two applicants for a job, equally qualified, the lighter is likely to get it. Dark girls are at a disadvantage in finding upper class husbands. The old myth is still believed. The gap is still there but, provided the dark skinned have money to purchase education and provided they accept the power of Christ which builds interior goodness, they can today find bridges across the chasm.

Another manifestation of the gulf is that the classes

speak excellent English; while the masses speak Jamaican patois. Less than 5 per cent of the population speaks standard English habitually and naturally in the homes. More than 95 per cent speaks the dialect. The ability to speak good English is a treasured possession and is guarded against the tendency "to slip down into the degraded language of the masses".

All public functions are conducted in precise English —more precise than that used in North America. Sermons, speeches, hymns, prayers, teaching, essays in schools, answers in examinations—all these are in standard English. But the language in which the masses work, love, mourn, and fight is patois. It is a vivid language full of color and idiom. It expresses shades of meaning with accuracy. Thus it comes about that the official language for the Christian Faith, thoroughly natural for the classes, is an artificial "put on" thing for the masses. It is the way successful, upper class people talk. For the masses, "right" tends to be a thing "they" talk about in church. It has little relation to what really counts in the hurly burly of earning a living, man-woman relationships, or the crises of life.

The classes, through their monopoly of the secondary school and university education, have a sure grip on privilege. They have property. They have the magic light color. They have money. And, perhaps most significant, they have the only language which counts. To climb into the classes, a child of the masses must buy enough education to forget his mother tongue and learn a new language.

The classes and the masses, despite the sharp cleavage described, merge into one another. Sometimes the light skinned are the dregs and dark skinned socially se-

cure. There are men of little education and considerable
public acclaim.   Yet, by and large, there are and will
remain the privileged few and the underprivileged many—
the rulers and the ruled.   A middle class is developing to
be sure.   When it has grown to twenty per cent of the
population and men of the masses receive only slightly less
pay than teachers and ministers, the gulf we have described
will have been filled; but at present it is a prominent part
of the demographic picture.

II.   Class-Mass Society and Church Growth.

How does this social structure affect the nature and
growth of the Churches?

The Presbyterians, Methodists and Anglicans are
Churches of the Classes. The Baptists, who 150 years ago
championed the slaves, the Moravians, the Brethren, and
Disciples of Christ are Churches of the Masses, but their
leadership and public worship is solidly upper class.   The
Churches of God, Adventists, Pentecostals, and Churches
of Christ are Churches of the Masses, with leadership
largely from the masses. Overlapping occurs quite widely.
Many uneducated peasants and laborers are communicants in upper class Churches and some cultured men and
women are members of Churches of the masses.

Because the Church is so largely identified with the
upper classes, Christianity is widely confused with culture.
It is popularly considered more necessary to wear shoes,
stockings, and hats to church than to worship in spirit and
truth or to be a dedicated disciple.   To be Christian is
to behave like the upper classes.   Church meetings
are conducted with great decorum and reserve.   The language of the church is prayer-book English.   Free prayer

in patois—the language of the heart—by a person of the masses would be heard with patronizing little smiles and embarrassed titters.

Do the masses feel that the Churches are really theirs? Well, as we have seen, probably fourteen out of fifteen adults of the masses are actively out of the old-line Churches. This in a generally Protestand land.

If the Churches are to win the masses, reorientation is required. They must champion the causes of the masses. They must fight for educational opportunity for the masses. They must identify themselves with the masses. They must find ways to make Christianity active in patois, to make it perfectly natural and common to pray, preach, and sing in patois. Poorly dressed children, men, and women must feel perfectly at home in the churches. Many of the common people must be trained to be lay and clerical leaders. We need working class ministers who staunchly refuse to separate themselves from their people either culturally or financially. The Churches must make sure that the handicaps of the masses—educational, linguistic, economic, and political—do not debar them from full respected participation in and leadership of the congregations of the land.

We need ministers with an active social conscience— men who demand breaking up of the great estates and a distribution of land in five acre lots to the landless, who plead for scholarships in secondary schools and colleges specifically for children "whose parents own no land and have no education", and who agitate for school buildings for the masses fully as good as those now provided for the classes. To visit the country schools is a revelation. Many a church building, about 30 by 70 in size, houses an elementary school with an enrollment of 300 and more—eight full classes.   Even when government erects new buildings in the country, these provide one room for several classes. The confusion, noise, and over-crowding contrast sharply with provision made for upper class children in Kingston.

Cordial appreciation of the tentative attempts of the government and the Churches to lift the masses by providing them with better educational and health facilities and better pay should not obscure the deep wide gulf between the "haves" and the "have nots" which is a vivid part of the total picture. The gulf constantly conditions the structure and growth possibilities of the Churches.

III. A Side Light from Brazil.

The International Missionary Council in 1943 published a study of the Church in Brazil done by Dr. Merle Davis which speaks to the problem of church growth in a class-mass society.

The population of Brazil numbered 45,000,000. Of these, 450,000 belonged to the upper classes, 1,000,000 to the "middle" classes, and 43,550,000 to the masses. If we list the upper and "middle" classes together, we see that three per cent of the population belonged to the classes and ninety seven per cent to the masses. The masses were 70% illiterate. "They are" wrote a Brazilian quoted by Davis, "underfed and ragged. They are tortured by syphilis, tuberculosis, and leprosy, rendered lazy by verminosis and malaria.   Unconscious of their ignorance, suffering from the effects of drink, they are the prey of their more fortunate brothers who neglect and despise them. They live, but have no ambition nor incentives to progress." Dr. Davis says more judiciously, "The feudal organization of society, concentrating power and opportunity in the hands of the few and condemning the many to helplessness, has established a tradition of social apathy and low living standards."

While the classes (a million and a half) are well to do, the masses (forty-four million) are very poor. "The masses cannot buy bread, butter, milk, and meat. They live on starchy roots, black beans, manioc, and occasionally salt fish and bananas. Their earning power limits their participation in those intellectual experiences which make up the content of civilized life. The almost prohibitive cost of books and newspapers places a heavy handicap on a working man acquiring a higher standard of life, new ideas, better education, and an intelligent participation in democratic institutions."

All who have worked with the masses anywhere will recognize these characteristics. With some differences in degree they mark the masses in many countries. This is the way most of mankind has lived and with minor improvements, continues to live.

Jamaica, of course, is not Brazil. The English heritage is not the Portuguese. The Protestant Church is not the Roman Catholic. And the tight little island is not vast undeveloped Brazil. Yet the economic, educational, linguistic, and religious gap occurs in both lands. Davis' insights about Brazil have a bearing in Jamaica, and indeed, wherever a deep gulf separates the masses from the classes.

He points out, for example, how difficult it is for a congregation of the masses to pay the salary required by a middle class minister. He says "the masses in Brazil are living close to the subsistence level. The appearance in their midst of a (middle class) family of non-producers whom they must support (at a middle class level) is a disaster. It upsets the economic balance of the community and introduces a way of life entirely outside their experience. The Evangelical Church as brought to Brazil is a middle class institution and requires the economic margin for support that is provided by the incomes of the middle class."

Davis states the case with restraint. He speaks about a "middle class", which in fact comprises that 2% of the population located at the very top of society, being the 97th and 98th per cent of the population. How western terminology leads us astray! Middle classes, which are really middle in the English or American sense, are almost non-existent in class-mass society.

Again he points out with great perspicuity that the rural pastor (i.e. the pastor of the masses) "should be able to share with his parishoners the customary type of house and some aspects of the basic forms of livelihood by which his people support themselves. He and his family must share in the simplicity of living, the discipline, and some of the processes that make up the world of his people. Otherwise he remains a privileged character, a person set apart, who looks at his people from the outside. He will find difficulty even in speaking the language of his people and winning their full confidence."

The emotionalism of the masses, Davis thinks, ought to be captured and used for Christ. For the masses, the cultured reserve of the classes is a thin chilly way of life. Quiet decorum is insipid fare after the spicy diet to which the working classes are accustomed. Davis says, "The typical Brazilian is endowed with a warmth and vigor of feeling which makes the colder-blooded Northerner seem sluggish and inhibited......Emotionalism in Brazilian Christian life is apparent in all denominations. An attention amounting to complete absorbtion in the service; a desire to participate; a loosing of self consciousness in the hearty response to a song, prayer, or exhortation; a natural behaviour in church; a reverence and evidenced emotion when stirred—these things are cumulative and make a unique impression."

He describes a Sunday meeting in a Pentecostal church thus. "There was prayer, Bible reading, and hymn singing. A period of impassioned prayer was led by the pastor and members from the congregation. The whole company prayed together, groaning, ejaculating, and repeating the sentences of the leader. The sound of innumerable voices rose to God, but all was orderly and controlled. After a few minutes the praying ceased. A man came to the pulpit and gave an intelligent inspirational witness to Christ's power in his own life. This received the closest attention of the congregation. These hundreds of underprivileged people found a release from the drabness of their lives in the various channels of emotional expression provided by the service....Those denominations are growing the fastest which recognize the emotional inheritance of the people and are giving it full opportunity for expression."

Davis goes on to say, "In the Church, lower class people enter a world of discipline, relationships, obligations, and fellowship different from anything they have experienced. They join a brotherhood of people who, like themselves, have tasted the bitterness of life and share in the hope of a redemption from the limitations of the old social and moral order......For people of the masses, the contrast between the way they have left and that they have entered is so complete that there are few inhibitions to "going all out" in witness, in contributing to church funds, and in participating in the whole church program. Here we find a secret both of the economic strength of these churches and of their rapid extension."

"The Pentecostal churches have evolved a practical leadership. Pastors come from the humble classes and are given a series of institute training courses, usually alternating periods of preaching with periods of study. The Pentecostal Church frankly is not seeking to attract the upper class Brazilian. The simplicity of its pastoral training is adapted also to a rapidly expanding Church. The many small congregations formed are not left without leadership, but are given direction and a sense of cohesion with the Brotherhood which keeps them from disintegrating. Such humble leaders can live on an economic level which would be impossible for highly trained men."

While the locus is Brazil in the above, Dr. Davis's remarks apply to the extension of the Church among the masses in general. Churchmen of various Churches, working among the masses anywhere would do well respectfully to study the record in Brazil and learn how to adapt secrets of success there—in those Churches which have grown vigorously—to their own populations.

IV. Upper Class Leaders and Church Reproduction Among the Common People.

Despite all we have just said, the leadership of some younger Churches, in Brazil and elsewhere, both lay and clerical, is composed of educated men and women. It is notably so in Jamaica. Between the vast bulk of the population and the church leaders yawns the gulf—of income, education, influence, and world view. This gulf is likely to widen with the passing of the years, for the classes can be counted on to take the lion's share of any increase in standard of living which the future may bring.

The younger Churches too, to satisfy their own members and to achieve parity in their dealings with the older Churches must have some highly educated ministers. Hence their seminaries strive for standards which compare favorably with those of the great seminaries of the West. The Theological Education Fund of the International Missionary Council assists them. This is good; but the cultural gulf between ministers so trained and the great majority of their own people, both Christians and the multitudes yet to become disciples of Christ, becomes deeper and wider than ever.

Of course, every minister seeks to be a friend and servant of the common people. He meets all classes—at dedications, baptisms, weddings, and funerals, in pastoral calling, and around community problems. He visits the sick. He teaches the youth. He talks with the men. He prays with all. More than any other professional man, he crossses the gulf. Yet, educated tastes, upper class mores, and higher standards of living, do separate ministers from people. They handicap personal relations with the common people. The kind of houses ministers live in, the language they speak, the food they eat, and the clothes they wear set them apart from the masses. Ministers quite naturally like to be with their own sort, so their leisure tends to be spent with them. Their own upper class standards also help determine the kind of worship, theology, hymnology, and religious education provided in the churches.

Church or mission schools play a large part in this

process. They enlist the children of the financially and intellectually more able. They give them the key to the classes. They thus create a new middle class highly useful to any developing nation. Out of this new middle class come leaders of the churches and those intellectual and spiritual giants who form the inter-continental leadership of the Church. But, good as all this is, Christian education also tethers the Church to the upper classes. They lead it. They control it. What they like by way of worship and teaching, they obtain. It is easy—though by no means inevitable—for them to become indifferent to the conversion and inclusion of "the great unwashed". They can also talk easily about the crying need to present Christianity to the upper classes.

This whole process often effectively seals a younger Church off to biological growth. It baptizes its own children; but from the outside, only those are eagerly sought and accepted whose children can be transformed by the Church's educational apparatus into middle class people.

In Jamaica we see a variant of this process. The schools of the Church have created the upper classes and put them in charge of the churches. But because the Island was technically Christian, the church schools have also imbued the masses with the rudiments of education and of Christian knowledge, so that when men win success in life, they come up out of a marginal relationship to the Church into full membership. The most earnestly Christian and devout among them often become influential in the old-line congregations. Yet the multiplication of the newer Churches of the masses is eloquent testimony that very large numbers of potential leaders still remain out of the Church How can we disciple the masses? What kind of a Church will hold in one fellowship both the classes and the vibrant new masses who will not follow meekly at their heels? These are important and unanswered questions.

In Jamaica, the cultural gulf constitutes a difficult problem for any Church concerned about the 800,000 adults who are out of the Church. Among younger Churches in other lands, facing dominant non-Christian religions, how a leadership of "middle class" Churches geared to the West can win the multitudes (peasants and laborers) is an even more difficult problem. The very things the educated nationals and missionaries feel are reverent, sensible, and "what our Church has always stood for" may be treasured upper class patterns impossible for the masses anywhere. They may have little to do with essential Christianity.

Jamaican churches show how chasms in culture affect church growth. Let us see how this is so. Elsewhere, failure to grow is commonly ascribed to non-Christian opposition, which, in some cases, may truly be the chief cause. But in Jamaica, growth is arrested not by opposition but, at least in part, by the gulf we have described. Other lands might ask whether this same gulf is causing lack of growth in their own churches.

In Jamaica several Branches of the Church of God have achieved notable growth among the masses. The old-line Churches frequently express the opinion that the pastors of these multiplying congregations are "unlearned and ignorant men". Such pastors from among the people, earnest Christians but little educated, may be a *sine qua non* for growth among the masses. Luke implies in the words we have quoted that, compared with the Jewish upper classes, the apostles were "unlearned and ignorant"— men of the masses. Under their leadership, however, "multitudes were added to the Lord". At least we can be sure that, among the various ways of bridging the gulf, drawing ministerial leaders from the people who are turning to the Lord is one effective method.

However these matters be, it is clear that church growth in Jamaica must take place in a class-mass society, where the churches precisely because they have been successful in the redemption and uplift of their members, tend to become upper class, out of touch with the masses, a select company of the successful. The classes are relatively well churched. Huge numbers of the masses are out of the Churches. The old-line Churches are not winning them. Each Church should therefore ask itself, "What must we do, what changes must we institute, to make our churches indefinitely reproduceable *among the masses*? To fill our churches with the proletariat and make them genuine churches of the common man?"

This is a most crucial problem both in Jamaica and in other lands. In the battle between the classes and the masses, the masses are going to win. The future belongs to the common man. The Churches and their missions must not be or even appear on the side of the already defeated upper classes. Jesus Christ is the champion of the poor and oppressed. Passion for justice and brotherhood wells up in those He indwells. Whatever it entail and cost, His must become churches of fishermen, carpenters, publicans, sinners, ignorant and unlearned men. Blessed are the poor for theirs is the Kingdom of Heaven.

CHAPTER IV

THE DARK RIVER

I. Why Talk About It?

Any treatise on church growth in Jamaica to be realistic or helpful must deal factually with concubinage and illegitimacy.

The subject is discussed by many writers on the Church in Jamaica, but none we have seen explain its relation to the structure and growth of the churches. For example, Wilfred Easton, long a missionary in Jamaica, in his fine book, *West Indies' What of the Church*, 1950, writes: "Three out of four babies are born of unmarried parents. Faithful concubinage, which arose out of the inhuman treatment accorded slaves, takes the place of Christian marriage......Sex relations are considered simple and natural. Christian marriage is considered an expensive custom to be indulged in if you can afford it. The situation is not to be condemned outright as immoral......The important consequence is that this custom militates against the growth of family life." Here illegitimacy is dealt with as a delicate subject which it is discourteous to mention, and which in the light of history is quite understandable. This is well said, but casts no light on how concubinage affects the growth and welfare of the Church.

Merle Davis, whose 1942 book, *The Church in the New Jamaica*, is the best summary of conditions we have seen, discusses concubinage and illegitimacy in detail. He proves their extent and illustrates their nature. He quotes government reports giving eleven reasons for their prevalence. He describes their evil effects. They repudiate responsibility. They rear children with no semblance of home life. They breed poverty and pauperism. They place staggering burdens on the taxpayers and the whole economy. This also is true and well said, but casts little light on how illegitimacy conditions and determines the entire structure and growth patterns of the churches, affects their systems of Christian education, and largely neutralizes their evangelistic campaigns.

The subject is of such crucial importance to the increase of church membership that we shall deal with it at length. Let us be clear at the outset, however, that we speak of it neither as a moral blight on Jamaican character, nor as an indelicate subject to be mentioned with bated breath, but simply as one of the chief difficulties facing our churches. Only as it is seen and described accurately, can the Church take sensible measures to correct it, and free itself and Jamaica from the enormous handicap to progress which it imposes.

II. The Two Patterns of Marriage.

In an attempt to be objective, we shall avoid the traditional, loaded words—concubinage and illegitimacy. Since we write not to blame but to describe, we shall speak instead of Patterns I and II, Acts One, Two, and Three, and the Dark River. These terms are free of blame or scorn. They are accurate. They avoid lumping many relationships together under the one term "concubinage." They thus enable accurate thinking about this crucial, many-sided problem. Finally they illuminate the relationship of church growth to this whole subject.

There are two distinct marriage patterns in Jamaica,—Pattern I and Pattern II.

Pattern I is Christian marriage. Both young men and young women ideally remain virgins before marriage, wed after completing their education, and remain married till death do them part. They rear children who, because of their cultural ideals and convictions and of the example and teaching of their church and parents, continue to practice Pattern I and hand it on to their children.

Pattern I is used by consciously Christian individuals in the upper classes. However less than half the present communicant membership in Jamaica follow Pattern I. A considerable portion of the present 200,000 communicants have practiced Pattern II, believe in Pattern II as a reasonable Jamaican way of marriage, and will communicate Pattern II to their children. An estimate of 100,000 adults who practice Pattern I would be generous.

Pattern II is used by some wealthy, educated persons and by most low-income, uneducated laborers and peasants. It is the common pattern in Jamaica.

Pattern II has three Acts. Act One starts around 16 years of age with casual boy-and-girl affairs involving sexual intercourse. Some of these last for a day, others for a few weeks, and others for months.

In Act Two, unions arise, i.e., a girl has regular visits from her boy friend or couples start living together for sentimental or economic reasons. Both clearly understand that this arrangement will break up whenever either chooses. Some of these unions last a few months, others a few years, and some a lifetime. When unions break-up, children born of them stay with the mother or grandmother. They make up the "adopted children" so often met in churches. Many unions break up through quarrels and infidelity Many break up through migrant labor. Men shift from region to region in search of work and leave one woman and take another. Some couples are affectionate and secure enough so that the man, if away, sends back money; but in many cases the man supports the woman and his children only as long as he lives with her.

Act Three has two forms: The first is Act Three Single. After years of living with a series of partners, some people quit having intimate relationship with the other sex. They are through with the joys and sorrows, the excitement and monotony of Acts One and Two. They have had enough. Some for physical, some for economic, and some for Christian reasons, pass out of Act Two into Act Three Single.

The second is Act Three Married. In this stage, couples whose unions have proved successful get legally married. Custom ordains that marriage be a significant and costly affair. A man contemplating marriage builds a house, or "fortifies" it with furniture and bedding. He gives a feast complete with wedding cake and wine. He buys wedding clothes and a ring. The cost of such marriage rules it out for impecunious young men. Pattern II people do not get married and start life on a shoe string. They get married only after they have made some money, gotten settled, and can afford it. They seek a church wedding only after living together for years and proving that they can get along. With increasing age, more and more Act Two couples pass into Act Three Married. Thus many elderly Christians have lived out all three acts of Pattern II. They believe it is "a good Jamaican way."

Christians in good standing in churches have said to us, when something we said seemed critical of Pattern II, that being foreigners we could not understand the "Jamaican way." A minister told us he recently officiated at a wedding where a guest openly congratulated the groom on having sense enough to get married only after having children by the lady of his choice. Jamaican women who follow Pattern II widely believe that their "boy friends" treat them better if they (the women) can terminate the relationship at any time. Men believe that the women work better and give less trouble if they (the men) can walk out any time they please. Many women of Pattern II would, however, marry if the men concerned would agree. Men are more the cause of the pattern than the women.

It would be a mistake to assume that Pattern II is strictly Jamaican. An instructive parallel occurs in George Bernard Shaw's *Pygmalian*. Colonel Pickering asks Alfred Doolittle, a London proletarian who is living with his sixth kept woman, "Why don't you marry that missus of yours?" Doolittle replies, "Tell *her* so, Governor, tell her so. Its me that suffers by it. I've no hold on her. I got to be agreeable to her. I got to give her presents. I got to buy her clothes something sinful. I'm a slave to that woman, Governor, just because I'm not her lawful husband. And she knows it, too. Catch her marrying me!"

III. **The Statistical Base**.

What proportion of the population practices Pattern II? Readers allergic to figures had better skip this section, though it is essential to full understanding.

The following table is taken from George W. Roberts' excellent book, *The Population of Jamaica*, page 267. The whole book is full of meaning for Christian leaders.

Table I:—Distribution in Per Cents of the Population by Family Types

Age	Male			Female		
	Single	Common Law	Ever Married	Single	Common Law	Ever Married
15–19	99.5	.3	.2	93.0	5.3	1.7
20–24	86.6	3.3	10.1	65.6	23.6	10.8
25–34	49.9	29.2	21.0	42.3	29.0	28.7
35–44	27.6	30.5	41.9	33.6	22.0	44.4
45–54	22.7	22.3	55.0	33.9	11.1	55.0
55–64	20.6	13.1	66.3	33.1	4.4	62.5
65–	19.0	6.2	74.7	32.2	1.1	66.7

Note the following facts:

The extremely small number of "married" in the 15-19 and 20-24 year groupings. The large numbers listed for these groupings under "single" are (with a few exceptions, chiefly in the student category) in Act One.

The 29 per cent of all women in the island between 15 and 24 who live in "common law" unions. These are all in Act Two.

The slow steady rise of the percentages in the "married" columns. Everyone else is either in Act One, or

Act Two, or Act Three Single. Practically all the increase in the "married" above thirty years of age comes from Act Two getting married.

The 20-30 per cent of men age 35-75 and the 30-35 per cent of women of age 35-75 who remain "single." "Single" means for a few "chastely single," for others "promiscuously single," for others "temporarily single," and for still others Act Three Single —"widows," "widowers," or in short persons who are "through with the other sex." What the proportion of each is, there is no way of ascertaining. The chastely single believe in Pattern I and are firm church members. Elderly Act Three Single women, many with children or grandchildren, form a large percentage of the membership of many working class churches. The promiscuously or temporary single are practicing Act One, Pattern II and would not seek communicant membership in Evangelical Churches.

The proportion of more or less permanent unions (common law marriages) rises to be a peak of 30 per cent "of the population between 25 and 44 years of age." In this age group are 508,000 persons of whom 30 per cent (160,000 persons) live in permanent or semi-permanent unions. *There are more persons between the ages of 25 and 44 living in common law marriage than there are communicant members of the old-line Churches.* If the Churches could find some way to persuade them to accept Christian marriage, communicant membership could be more than doubled.

Most couples living in Act Two eventually get legally married—as the declining percentages in the middle columns abundantly indicate. The Church would be enormously strengthened if this occurred before they were thirty years old. Miss Clarke maintains that the lasting

unions are started in a different way from the temporary
unions. She therefore calls them "purposive unions".
The Church would gain if it could persuade those entering
purposive unions (i.e., where they intend to stay together)
to begin with Christian marriage.

Calculations based on G. W. Roberts' table, quoted a
few pages back, show that about 78 per cent of the total
population between the ages of 15 and 44 fall into the
"single" and "common law" classifications. Since there
are about 800,000 souls in Jamaica of this age grouping,
there are about 620,000 living in Acts One and Two.

According to Robert's book (page 61) 11 per cent
of the total population, i.e. about 180,000 persons, fall in
the 45-64 year age grouping. Of this number about
80,000 fall in the "single' and "common law" classifications. By adding 80,000 to 620,000 we get a total of
700,000 persons who are adherents of Pattern II.

To these should be added those who are married as
the Third Act of Pattern II—at least 100,000. Thus we
get at least 800,000 men and women above the age of 15
who are adherents of Pattern II.

As a check on this estimate we use another procedure.
There are about 1,000,000 persons in Jamaica above the
age of 14. We saw that 100,000 was a liberal estimate for
adherents of Pattern I. And there are some chastely single.
Thus there must be 800,000 to 900,000 adherents of Pattern
II.

IV. Some Bearings on Church Membership.

This very common marriage pattern brings it about
that in most rural congregations *"Christians over forty"*
comprise three fourths or more of the membership,—Act Three

Marrieds and Singles. Both groups are made up of people who have lived for years with one or more partners. The singles come out of the experience alone. The married have legalized the last union they were in. Both are now eligible to join the church and generally do so.

Both have children and often grandchildren who were born in and have grown up in Pattern II. Their neighbors, relatives, and intimates, with whom they must get along, are in many cases living in Pattern II. Like Alfred Doolittle's missus, they discern many real advantages in it. Church members are thus caught in a conflict of loyalties. As Christians they believe Christian marriage is good. As followers of Pattern II, they also believe that "Christian marriage is scarcely practical for our people". Deacons and elders sometimes have their own children living with them in Acts One and Two.

Hence Christians have evolved the compromise solution we have described—Christian marriage as Act Three, i.e. Christian marriage without condemnation of or earnest striving against Acts One and Two.

Most congregations have in them adherents of Patterns I and II in varying proportions. In highly cultured urban congregations, many of I and a few of Act Three. In most rural churches, very few of I and most of Act Three.

Pattern II is true of the masses. It is less true of the classes. Of earnest Christians in the upper classes it is quite untrue. They are practicing Pattern I faithfully under difficult circumstances.

V. **The Dark River**.

We now change the figure from a drama to a river. There is a Dark River in Jamaica. It engulfs most young people. Let us see how. Children go to Sunday School and church, and to government and parochial schools. They are as responsive, intelligent, and good as children anywhere in the world. At the onset of puberty, youth in Pattern II homes largely cease coming to church and Sunday School. Adolescence affects day school pupils also. "Sexual maturity", says Miss Clarke, "may abruptly terminate school life even before the normal school-leaving age." In rural churches people of 15 to 35 years of age are scarce. Most young people of 15 to 18 go down into the Dark River. There they stay till, at the age of 30 to 50, by the earnest labors of Christians, the operation of the Holy Spirit, and the social advantages of the legally married state, a proportion emerge. This never-ending procession of children of God marching down into the Dark River in the prime of life, many of them never to emerge, is a large part of the problem of church growth in Jamaica.

In passing, we note a similar but much smaller dip in active church memberships in North America among older young people, particularly men who do not get married. A priest said, "They begin making bad confessions and soon make none at all." Evangelicals note college students and working men who "lose interest in the church". Among other causes of the dip, sex practices which make persons uncomfortable in the worship of the Triune God probably play a large part. The Church everywhere loses when its young people do not get married. A large proportion of "youth which does not get married" will go down into some kind of a Dark River and out of the Church. Jamaica's problem arises because of environmental factors which operate everywhere. It does not arise

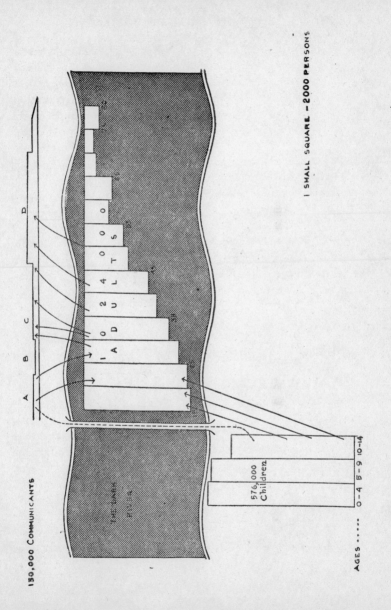

1 SMALL SQUARE = 2000 PERSONS

130,000 COMMUNICANTS

THE DARK RIVER

10 ADULTS 2400000

576,000 Children

AGES..... 0-4   5-9   10-14

A   B   C   D

of age) *in* the River. For Jamaica as a whole the pro-
portionate size of each section is accurate. There are in
Jamaica today 576,000 persons under 15 years of age and
1,024,000 persons above 14 years of age. They are distri-
buted exactly as shown in these 16 sections. The numbers
in the age groupings, for the hillside communities surround-
ing rural churches, are very like these. For example, during ages 20-30, the population is 17 squares deep, while
church membership is half a square deep, i.e. for every person in the church, there are *over* 30 out of the church. But
in the 55-65 year group, for every person in the church
there are only two and a half out of it.

3. The Communicants. The *spread* of communicant members (given above the Dark River) is based on
actual age distributions in four typical rural churches. The
spread therefore accurately depicts the age grouping of
a hillside membership, and probably of most hillside
memberships.

Its *area* is to the total area of the pyramid as 116,000
(total communicants of old-line Churches in Jamaica) is
to 1,600,000 (total population of Jamaica).

4. The Bridge. A proportion of Christian youth
(very small in churches of the masses but larger in upper
class churches) crosses the Dark River into communicant
membership on the *bridge of upper class standards, Christian
instruction, conversion, or advanced schooling*. The dotted line
represents this very small proportion going across the
bridge directly into communicant membership. Youth
work in the churches increases this proportion.

The River flows on darkly from the past into the
future. *A very large per cent* of Jamaican youth marches
down into the River, generation after generation. Till it

comes out, either by getting legally married at an advanced age or by resolving to have no further sex relations, *it is automatically excluded from the church.*

Around each church, children under 15 comprise about six-sixteenths of the community. Look at the huge block on the lower bank: Note the great numbers of them compared with the communicants. Remember that most of these children will not become communicant members. Many of these children are in Christian Sunday Schools. Over two-thirds of those between 7 and 14 are in church day schools. Yet most of them never get across the Dark River.

They do not move into the Dark River—precisely at 15 years of age, of course. The graph might better have shown the 15-19 block half in and half out.

Even those who cross the bridge are not safe. Some teen age communicants have boy-and-girl affairs, contract temporary unions, and quit coming to Church and Sunday School. When such conduct is known, through pregnancy or otherwise, the secretary of the church writes "fallen away" after the name on the roll. In rural churches, unless the young communicant goes on to secondary school or teacher training, the Dark River usually gets him. This "falling away" is visually expressed in the arrows leading back into the Dark River. Many, who were baptized (or confirmed) between the ages of 10 and 16 and who account for Section A of the communicants, fall away, leaving a *very thin* Section B.

In the late twenties, a few conjugal unions (through conversion, persuasion by Christians, considerations of love or respectability, or by climbing up into the middle class) decide to get married and unite with the church.

The up-going arrows show these. As time goes on, more and more Act Two couples accumulate enough money and are sure enough of each other to get married. They begin Act Three Married and frequently come into the fellowship of the Church.

In the same age brackets other men and women decide that they are through with sex and become Act Three Singles. They also join the church or come back into communicant membership.

See sections C and D of the graph.

VI. What Does the Church Do About the Dark River?

The Church condemns the Dark River. She refuses membership to those already in it and excludes such communicants as fall into it.

The churches conduct Sunday Schools and day schools. They establish young people's societies and hold youth conferences. They run Daily Vacation Bible Schools and maintain church-managed secondary schools. Wherever a strong youth program goes into effect, larger numbers cross the bridge into full membership. (A very careful study needs to be made of adolescents who have become baptized Christians to discover how many of them stay out of the River and what factors help them to do so. We suspect from what we have seen and heard that (almost) only those stay out who are middle class or who, through education, become middle class. If further study confirms this suspicion, we should rectify the situation. It is unthinkable that the Church should resign itself to excluding all those who do not have money enough to go on to high school).

The churches through their ministers and members are continually searching for couples in the Dark River who can be converted, persuaded to marry, be baptized, and join the church. By pleading with friends, by mass marriages, by loaned wedding garments, by financial help, free ministerial services, and gifts of wedding rings, Christians work faithfully to rescue as many as possible. These labors bring reward. Starting from about thirty years of age, many couples whose temporary unions are proving satisfactory, one by one, accept Christ or are reinstated, and thus come into the church.

Christians in general sincerely believe Pattern II to be a bad thing. Those in concubinage, they say, are "living unbecoming." They have "fallen away." They are "in danger of eternal punishment." They are "unsaved." This conscience of Christians is partly shared by the unchurched also.

Coupled with this conscience, however, is a widespread feeling that Pattern II is inevitable. Convinced Christians will not grant that it is inevitable. That would be to limit the power of God and would be contrary also to their experience that those soundly converted do turn from their sins, get married, and start living right. But, nevertheless, Pattern II seems unavoidable. They say, "It is bad, but it is human nature. We don't like it, but what can we do about it?" With some, this is coupled with a feeling that Jamaicans are different, have a warmer nature, and are by heredity irresponsible. "These arrangements suit our young people who have to search for jobs. We are poor people, you know. This is the best we can do." The economic aspect was brought out by one who said, "He can only get married, Sir, if his father will build him a house. And the old people don't do that."

VII. **Where Does Pattern II Touch the Life of the Churches?**

It touches it at many places. Consider evangelism. If in an evangelistic meeting fifty confess Christ, the first task is to find out how many the church can accept and how many she cannot. She can accept: unmarried youth on the bank of the River, single men and women of any age (if truly single), and couples who are willing to get married. She cannot accept: converted men or women whose partners are unwilling to wed, and single men and women, young or old, who expect to enter or continue in a temporary union.

Consider the baptism (or in paedobaptist Churches, the confirmation) of adolescent boys and girls. The minister knows that, except for those with money enough to go on to higher schools, most of them will "fall away." Hence there is considerable sentiment in some churches for not baptizing or confirming working class youth, since this so often entails the pain and shame of later exclusion. It is like getting young people to sign that they will never drink liquor in a society where very many of them will (have to) break their pledge.

Consider infant baptism or dedication. Denominations which sprinkle infants have what, at first sight, is an advantage here. By sprinkling they make the infants part of their Church. Thus they get a large "Christian community". Of the small number confirmed, the working class youth tend to fall away. An upper class church arises, surrounded by a large community of chiefly lower class people, who "belong" to this church but are not eligible for full membership. Of this community, the most successful marry and join the church at an advanced age. At second glance, however, serious disadvantages are discovered. By sprinkling infants born out of wedlock on the ground that "the children must not suffer for the sin of the parents" the Church in effect condones Pattern II. By letting those sprinkled grow up and enter casual or purposive unions, while still considering themselves Presbyterians, Anglicans, Moravians, or Methodists (in short, Christians), the denomination lowers its standard and confuses the issue.

In the Christian Church (Disciples) debate rages as to whether or not it should dedicate babies born out of wedlock. Some ministers firmly believe it should not. The Duke Street Church explains to a mother who brings her baby to be christened that:—

christening is a pledge to rear the child a Christian;

if such a pledge is given, God will bless the baby;

only in a Christian home can a parent make such a pledge;

hence the minister cannot dedicate a baby whose parents are unmarried; so he will help the parents get married so they can have their lovely child christened in church and rear him as a Christian.

Such an approach often leads mother and father into marriage and membership.

Some Christian Church ministers, however, take the other tack, that by dedicating a baby born out of wedlock they attach the mother (often in rural churches one of their own girls) more firmly to their community. She will on occasion attend and contribute. If she and her man (this one or the next) ever marry they will join the Christian church. In the meantime the two and six dedication fee is additional church income. Conversely, if a minister refuses to christen, the mother will take the baby to another church, pay two and six to its minister, and consider herself a part of its community. The very strangeness of the sound of these paragraphs to English and American ears is eloquent testimony to the different situation churches face in Jamaica.

Consider exclusion from the Church for slipping into Pattern II. The Seventh Day Adventists take the sternest and most consistent Christian position here. They exclude not only members living in concubinage but even parents or grandparents who house dependents living in concubinage. The Adventists appear to prosper on this policy. They lose a few of their youth but, I am told, have a fine lot of young people in their churches and are rearing a Household of God which from generation to generation practices Christian marriage.

There are other bearings of Pattern II on the churches in Jamaica. Enough has been said, however, to indicate its wide ramifications.

VIII. What Kind of Church Growth Can We Expect with Pattern II?

We are thinking primarily of village and hillside churches, since they are so much more numerous than Kingston churches. Let us look back at the 130,000 communicants, represented by the long thin age grouping above the River. This picture represents the membership-age spread in a typical church....Exact understanding of this narrow strip, including ways into it and out of it, is necessary to see what quality, kind, and amount of church growth is possible for our congregations.

Further study of rural membership is needed. Life histories at several levels would be most helpful: (1) of each member to show when and how he came into the church and how long he stayed; (2) of each child in our communities to show what fraction of the total child community we get in Sunday Schools, and what happens to those influenced enough to stay on into the 12-15 year old classes and go to Young People's Conferences and Christian Youth Fellowships; and (3) of each communicant 10-24 years of age to find out what has happened to him or to her.

The same study would also be revealing in city churches of the masses.

Yet the following statement can be put forward tentatively. This is what people tell me, what church rolls and age distributions susbstantiate, and what in view of the whole picture seems reasonable.

Let us expand the diagram of the communicant membership above the Dark River.

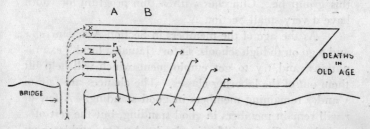

DARK RIVER

Note that the church is built up from two sources:

because of African descent.   In Jamaica the factors have united without opposition, that is all.

Universal knowledge of contraceptives, shortly to become a reality, whether we like it or not, will have a profound effect at this point all over the world.   Unmarried youth will be able to have sexual intercourse without the girl getting pregnant and hence without society knowing that sexual intercourse is going on.   Chaste courting will closely resemble in all observable facets courting with sexual intercourse.   The difference between courting and, as they say in the vernacular, "courting a storm" will be impossible for other people to discern.   Will the Church— hoping for the best—welcome and maintain as leaders unmarried youth who "date" freely?   If so, among her own children, how can she prevent a period of promiscuity prior to marriage?   Whatever answers to these questions the future may provide, they serve to show that the Dark River is not exclusively a Jamaican stream.   It also is a preview of conditions which in some countries will come about and in others have come about.

The accompanying diagram illustrates the relationship of the Dark River to the growth and welfare of the Church.   The diagram consists of four main parts.

1.   The Dark River itself.   This means the acceptance and practice of Pattern II, which in Acts One and Two *automatically exclude from the Church.*

2.   The Population Pyramid, given by Roberts on Page 61 of his book.   This shows the percentage of the total population in each age group.   We lay the pyramid on its side.   We put the first three sections (children below fifteen years old) on the lower bank of the River.   We put the next thirteen sections (i.e., persons 15 to 80 years

those who first cross the bridge and enter membership
as virgins; and those who later come up from the River
to accept Christ.

Note that bridge crossers (dotted arrows) are made
up of several kinds of youth—x, y, z, r, and p—These class
distinctions are essential to understanding.

x—youth of the upper classes, children of ministers,
teachers, etc.;

y—youth on their way up into the upper classes via education; and

z—working class youth who will till the land or be servant
girls or do casual labor in the towns and cities.

Of "z" are some whom we shall call

r—sons and daughters of landowners who never hire themselves out to others; and some, whom we shall call

p—sons and daughters of small peasants or landless labor
(or the children of their daughters).

All these (x, y, z, r, and p) during the years 13 to 19
(Section A) will attend youth fellowships, go to youth conferences, and sit in Sunday School classes. The more
vigorous the youth program of a church, the larger will
this group be. Churches with a thin program for youth
have a very small Section A.

As the age of the members in Section A advances, x
and y go on to high schools, sit for "Jamaica local", examinations, and try to get employment which will help lift
them out of the laboring classes. The chances are fair of
x and y remaining members in good standing. A few of
r will remain members in good standing, but the rest of r
and almost all of p will begin playing Act One and later on
Act Two. Beside their names on the roll will be written
"fallen away."

Therefore Section B (ages 20 to 29) in many churches is very thin. Late in B a few couples are added. From about the age of 35 more and more are added, both couples and single men and women who intend to live according to the Christian code. Occasionally some of them also drop back into the River.

What will happen if a church presses forward with fervent work and evangelism *among youth*? More young persons will cross the bridge, but the nature of the ingathering will be different in each social class x to p. We consider them one by one.

Of x the church will get most of the upper class youth in its congregation. This means many for some city congregations; but very few for most rural congregations for very few upper class people live in the open countryside.

Of y the church will also get only a few because education is expensive. Evangelism or a youth program will lift out of z into y only those whose parents can pay the cost of education. If the Church plus the Missionary Society helps boys and girls go to school (providing school busses, building high schools near its churches, granting scholarships, and pre-seminary stipends for ministerial students, and the like) then, *with abundant evangelism*, class y will increase and remain in the church.

Of z the church will get many into the membership—chiefly girls, however. But since the Church has no present goal of getting its working class youth happily married before they are 18, most young members, after a period in the communicant membership, will march down into the Dark River. "Their chances of falling away are very good, indeed," said more than one minister to us.

The more the outcome of evangelism is "joining the

church" and the less it is "radical conversion," the greater the loss here. Even the radically converted "fall away" on occasion, however. The more complete the surrender to Christ, the more truly the convert is filled with the Holy Spirit, and the more the Church believes that the Christian is truly a "new creation," the less the loss. Each minister might make the presence of this age group *from amongst working class youth* the test of whether he is preaching a vital redeeming gospel.

What will happen if a church presses forward with earnest *adult evangelism* and *adult church work?* It will enlarge the number of rescued persons represented by the solid arrows going up into the communicants. These rescued people include men and women of different ages and status groupings; as we can see from two accompanying "Distributions". These take the complete memberships of four small churches—147 communicants—and classify them according to age and status.

Age Distribution 12–24 25–39 40–49 50–59 60 and up Total
No. of members   17   16   51   41   22   147

Status Distribution

	members
Full families, both married, both members, elderly	44
Half families, married, but only one member elderly	7
Single women above 40	54
Single men above 40	9
Single women 20-39	16
Single men 20 to 39	7
Teen age girls	9
Teen age boys	1
	Total 147

In the Age Distribution, the figures, 16, 41, 51 represent the net result of much past adult evangelism. The greatest response is in those above forty. The same fact can be seen in the Status Distribution, where 114 are "elderly" or "above 40."

At King's Gate—a city church—during the last three years adult evangelism brought in 103 persons, of whom about 70 were couples of under forty. This indicates that the 25 to 39 year old group is a fruitful one to approach. It is a large part of all populations and fewer of its members have already been persuaded, converted, and married.

These rescued couples and middle-aged single women represent solid gains. Their chances of remaining in the church are good. On the other hand, some ministers feel that when joining the church is put on such a human basis (get married, quit "living unbecoming", achieve status for yourself and your children) " "converts" do not make fervent Christians.

Thus church growth through "evangelism and vigorous program" has its limitations. Returns are small compared with efforts.

Let us put the same truth in other words. The Church in general is the institution of the small, highly privileged classes, largely because only in the classes does the marriage pattern allow youth to remain in the communicant membership. It might almost be said that "in the lower classes (who comprise 90 per cent of the population) the Church exists only by virtue of Act Three and elderly single women." There are, of course, exceptions—the younger "real Christians," or "genuinely converted"— who, though of the working classes, live chaste lives before marriage at whatever age that comes, or whether it ever comes or not. Quite likely some denominations which stress individual regeneration and have sufficient discipline have many such and other denominations have few. Before a true quantitative statement can be made, much careful research needs to be done.

IX. Could the Churches Liquidate Pattern II?

We believe they could. Just as, a hundred and fifty years ago, they launched a long desperate battle with slavery, so today the Churches could determine to wipe out Pattern II.

This is an auspicious time to do it. The revolution is affecting all of life in Jamaica. Old patterns of labor and social relationships, unchallenged since emancipation, are being revised. Dark skinned people are now freely employed in business offices. Labor unions are growing stronger. Widespread changes in the framework of society are under way.

On the day I am writing these pages, the *Gleaner* of Kingston carries a two column story about West Indian girls in London. In it the Lord Bishop of Jamaica (a Jamaican) says, "The English are horrified at the prevalence of common law wives among the West Indian communities in London." Here is a new factor in the situation —world opinion. The whites who ruled Jamaica during the last 200 years, regarding concubinage as a degrading custom liked by what they considered an inferior race, were indifferent to world opinion about Jamaicans. But today's rulers, being Jamaicans themselves, will, we believe, hotly resent low opinion of Jamaicans and take steps to eradicate what causes it. They do not believe it is natural to or good for Jamaicans. In this new day the Churches can lead the new Jamaica to liquidate this evil spawn of slavery which so heavily handicaps all efforts at progress and which so stigmatizes the Island.

To be sure, the task will be difficult. Pattern II is firmly entrenched. Edith Clarke's *My Mother Who Fathered Me* shows how the accepted system of land tenure, the conditions of labor on sugar estates, and in factories, the living conditions of most domestics, and the legal structure of the country combine to make Pattern II very strong. It is as strong as slavery—perhaps stronger since the masses believe it is a good system, suitable for them.

Eradicating Pattern II cannot be done by any amount of general Christian education of children on the banks of the River, plus any amount of evangelism designed to rescue some out of the Dark River. The whole pattern itself, with the values and judgments which support it, must be rejected by the Churches.

Such rejection does *not* involve utopian outlawing adultery or forbidding mistresses to the rich. These debasing practices are found abundantly even in lands where Christian marriage is the accepted rule. Even after Pattern II has been eliminated in Jamaica, adulteries, unfaithfulness, and the vices of the rich will be as common as they are in the United States. No one should confuse such sins with Pattern II.

Rejection of Pattern II concerns solely rejection of the *accepted* postponement of marriage till financial success has been achieved while at the same time sexual intercourse is carried on with sundry partners. We are not speaking about lapses in conduct; but about accepting Pattern II as normal. Public opinion, including much Christian public opinion, holds that marriage *should be* or even must be postponed for the impecunious sons and daughters of the masses. A job, a house, clothes, furniture, rings, income, and status are held to be more necessary for proper marriage than youth and virginity.

Before Pattern II is destroyed, getting sons and daughters suitably married before the age of twenty will have to become the accepted goal of Christian parents and congregations. Before Pattern II is destroyed, the masses in Jamaica will have to do like the masses in India and Africa and China do, and like those in Germany, America, England, and Scandinavia did before the industrial revolution—get their sons and daughters married, at about the age of sixteen for the girl and eighteen for the boy. Marriage should normally take place at sexual maturity, when the girl becomes a woman and the boy becomes a man. Postponement is immoral unless accompanied by parental and personal discipline sufficient to assure chastity during the period of waiting.

Those who immediately exclaim, "But this is financially impossible in Jamaica", merely emphasize that they are thinking about marriage from the ruler class point of view. It is indeed, impossible to have a million dollar wedding on a ten dollar income. It is quite possible, however, to have a ten dollar wedding. Hundreds of millions of such marriages are celebrated every decade among the common people of earth.

Let us approach the question negatively? If early marriage for youth of the masses is not the solution, what is? Can we believe that working class youth can be so educated, converted, and set to work in the churches, that very large numbers of them will remain unmarried—

and communicants in good standing—till they are financially successful?

We are driven to the conclusion that under the conditions which face Jamaican Churches, *only widespread early marriage, with Christian character and home training deep enough to make it succeed, will enable Pattern II to be eliminated.* The middle clause is fully as important as the first.

X. What Can Churches Do Now?

1. Preaching the gospel of salvation is essential.

Calling on men and women to repent of their sins, believe on the Lord Jesus Christ, be baptized in His name, and lead godly lives is the most important thing any church does. Nominalism of all sorts which permits frailties in church members as a matter of course, "to be expected of these people" is a deadly enemy. Proclamation of individual regeneration by the power of the Gospel, through genuinely reborn men and women is tremendously needed. Baptism or confirmation should not be a "normal experience for our adolescents" into which they "graduate" before Easter after a few lessons in the communicants' class, whether they really have fully surrendered to Christ, been converted, or not. Baptism should be the sign of dying to sin and rising to new life through conscious, fervent faith. Confirmation should be most meaningful.

Nothing written in succeeding paragraphs should leave the impression that Pattern II can be wiped out by mechanical devices, graded courses of instruction, human ingenuity, or persistence. Sound conversion, being filled with the spirit of God, offering our bodies as a spiritual sacrifice, living a life of continual communion with Christ the power of God to salvation is urgently needed. The presence of numbers of young working class Christians in churches which stress total surrender and holy living is abundant proof that power to live victorious lives is available to all who become true disciples of Christ.

Every church should therefore continue seeking to win Act Two men and women to a Christ-filled state involving marriage and to win youth and adults not in Act Two to a Christ-filled state which involves chastity.

Visitation evangelism with its house-to-house teaching of and pleading with men and women to accept Christ, get married if they are couples, and live chastely if they are not, is already a common church activity. It can be intensified in many churches.

2.   Christian education is essential.

Sunday Schools and Youth Fellowships are present in most churches, though they are thin and weak where few 15-35 year olds are communicants. We need a much larger number of adolescent boys and girls in our classes and fellowships. Much more effort to get them in, keep them in, and win every one of them for Christ is urgently necessary.

This is equally true of adults. Greatly increased attendance of adults, particularly young adults, is urgent. Christians should study God's word. Communicant parents who go to Sunday School themselves will have the greatest success in getting their adolescents to attend.

The British or American produced programs of these educational organizations are much better than nothing. It is better to have youth and adults studying what Christianity means in Indiana or England than to have it studying nothing. And, where foreign materials and programs are used, the wide-awake minister can suggest adaptations to suit Caribbean Christians.

But the traditional programs, curricula, and materials for Christian education, produced as they are in America or Britain, are discouragingly foreign and upper class. They do not speak to the needs of working class Jamaican Christians. They do not deal with what being Christian means to the employed and unemployed on these hillsides. They do not speak about Acts One and Two and the Dark River. They do not point out that Act Three may be either gloriously Christian or a worldly compromise.

Jamaican materials, however, could speak effectively. They could aim to multiply the number (1) of working class youth dedicated to live in Pattern I with its normal early marriage, and (2) of working class mothers, grandmothers, and fathers dedicated to rearing children in Pattern I and getting them suitably married at an early age.

A whole series of educational procedures suggest themselves. A curriculum can be worked out on these themes, with appropriate textbooks and Bible lessons to support it. Courses can be planned at the Junior, Intermediate, and Senior level in which Pattern II will be described, its roots in slavery and oppression laid bare, its disadvantages exposed, and its degrading nature and wastage explained.

Youth organizations, assisted by church boards and councils, could lead Christian youth in all churches to pledge themselves to chastity before marriage, to marry shortly after completing their education (whether that be standard V, high school, or college) and to look for work in cities or countryside as Christian couples.

Adults could receive teaching on Christian family life, couched not in terms suitable to England or America (those knowing nothing but Pattern I), but in terms meaningful to those immersed in Pattern II. For example, to "small settler" Christian parents "Christian Family Life" for their 18 year old son means getting him married to a fine Christian girl, helping him build an inexpensive little house (may be just a booth), and making life pleasant for the new couple. If it does not mean this, it means nothing. Not to do this is to thrust the young man into Act One and out of the Church!

Post-baptismal courses for *converts from the working classes* are greatly needed and entirely lacking. They should be prepared on three levels: (1) adults (20-39 years old) who cannot read or who read with difficulty; (2) adults (20-39 years old) who read easily—4th standard passes or above; (3) teenagers who have decided for Christ, been instructed, and baptized.

Courses will be slanted to each level. In addition to the ordinary subjects of instruction, all will treat of chastity, Pattern II as the deceptive, destructive thing it is, ways of getting sons and daughters married before the age of twenty to suitable Christian partners, and ways in which Christian young people can themselves choose suitable partners. All will have lessons on the working class Christian home, and the husband-wife, father-child, and mother-child behavior in it.

Numerous tracts (needing some editing, to be sure) could be written by the happily married and published by the thousands. The authors, (Jamaican peasants, laborers, and small settlers) would tell of how satisfying Christian marriage is. They would relate how they turned from expensive, deceitful, slave Pattern II to the security of Pattern I, or how they arranged the marriage of their 18 year old sons and daughters happily.

Courses on Christian conduct in a world where knowledge of contraception is widespread are needed. Because of the population explosion governments will soon give everyone knowledge of how to cohabit without having children. Among those committed to Act I, this will mightily reinforce promiscuity. Among those committed to early Christian marriage, this will enable young couples to defer children till earnings permit them.

Other educational procedures will no doubt suggest themselves.

3. Direct Christian action and social legislation is essential.

The curse of Jamaica for three hundred years has been economic systems and government actions which exploited men regardless of family life. Slaves were work units—not persons. Marriages were forbidden—not celebrated. Slaves were sold or exchanged regardless of marital unions. Slaves were even bred like cattle. Female slaves were used and discarded by their masters. White men through customs, governmental regulations, and economic systems produced the iniquitous system of mating which grew into Pattern II. Slave owners vigorously resisted any change which might have given value to the persons involved. Temporary unions and casual mating were established as normal—for negroes, mulattos, quadroons, and any who had African blood in his veins.

After emancipation, the slaves were politically free, but the seat of economic power had not changed. Plantation owners and wealthy colored people still got their work done for pittance wages regardless of the marital status of their employed. They would have laughed at the idea that they were in any way responsible for honorable marriage among their "irresponsible, ignorant ex-slaves." Race prejudice stepped in to assist economic and legal pressures by suggesting that Africans liked casual sex and loose temporary unions. Legal or conventional systems of employment made casual sex seem necessary—even though uncounted thousands of devoted Christians among the small settlers and wage earners watched in agony while their unmarried daughters went out to work and came home pregnant.

The wealthy in Kingston and other towns (merchants, teachers, missionaries, government servants, doctors, clergymen, and business men) employed workmen, domestics, factory hands, and menials without asking whether those employed had the possibility of living as married people, or whether the housing provided such single employees encouraged or required loose temporary unions. In this they were, of course, well within both the law and the accepted code of conduct. Yet that they still do it today is a serious blemish. Miss Clarke's description of contemporary conditions in Surgartown (p. 91ff) is a terrific indictment of the Churches—even though she never once mentions them.

True, the vicious mating patterns, which 170 years of slavery had forced on the masses, seemed to be "liked" by the people. The economic system forged the chains of concubinage and the laboring classes wore them so long they became accustomed to them. Young men and women drifting in and out of cane fields, Panama, England, Kingston, and domestic jobs, themselves being born out of wedlock, thought it convenient to form loose unions when opportunity offered and to terminate them as they moved. They still think so.

Christians, despite the fact that they form the majority of the ruling classes, have not united to demand, frame, and pass laws which would rectify this situation. The Church has not yet angrily risen to destroy the economic, legal, and social framework which perpetuates Pattern II. Any such attempt will require both Direct Christian Action and Christian Social Legislation. It required this third factor to destroy slavery. It will require this third factor to destroy slavery's child.

To illustrate what we mean by Direct Christian Action, we quote Miss Clarke's *My Mother Who Fathered Me*, page 151: "A large number of our life histories record that invariably in these circumstances (ordinary domestic service in the centers studied) the girl seeks for a man who, in return for companionship and sexual favors, will give her presents of money, clothes and trinkets. When the inevitable pregnancy occurs, the girl has to leave her job but it is rare for the union to be stabilized......An overwhelming majority of women in domestic service throughout the Island are supporting or partially supporting children left in the care of a mother or other relative." An aroused social conscience among upper class Christians could lead many of them to employ only those for whom they can provide Christian living conditions. Individuals no doubt are already doing this, but there is no organized effort yet to pledge all upper class Christians to hire only married maids or married men servants and to do without servants rather than hire and house unsupervised single persons. Such direct action would be a mighty force for good in Jamaica.

Could churches build housing units in Kingston for young ruralites—to be available only to married communicants, and only for a few months while they looked for work? Could rural churches try to get their youth married before they set out to look for work?

During our stay in Jamaica, Miss Edith Clarke proposed a resolution—which passed—in the Legislative Council, making it mandatory for unmarried mothers to name fathers to the Registrar of births. This simple measure will not destroy Pattern II; but it fixes responsibility, is a long step in the right direction, and is, we hope, the first of other similar measures which will change the legal and economic framework and create a climate unhealthy for concubinage. A deduction by the employer on pay day of a portion of the wage of single men, for remittance to deserted wives and children would seem possible. Since the common man has the vote, low-cost governmental housing will become increasingly available. To give married couples first chance at such would appear desirable. Employers of domestics, factory hands, or cane field workers could be taxed a shilling a week for each single man or woman employed whose age was above eighteen. Divorce also can be made as readily available to the man earning ten pounds a month as to him who earns two hundred. These particular suggestions may not prove feasible, but Christians can devise and push through feasible social legislation which will provide a legal and economic framework favorable to Pattern I. More human working conditions, for example, if linked to a campaign to liquidate Pattern II would help.

A combination of these three factors—conversion, education, and social action—is likely to succeed. No one or two of them alone is sufficient. The trouble is that (1) the economic system still treats men and women as work units and expects them to form loose temporary unions which appear more convenient for employers, (2) class pride thinks the masses like Pattern II, (3) the law from the beginning has favored men and their sexual exploitation of women, and (4) helpless women and ill-educated peasant and laboring classes accept the situation. All four factors combine to perpetuate a pattern of sex relations thoroughly inimical to the Christian way of life. Individual converts are lifted out of the pattern, but their children slip back into it. Middle-aged men and women repent of their sins, get right with God, regularize their relationships, get married, and join the church, but they do not really renounce the pattern. They do not like the "falling away" but sadly expect it of the young people— their own children, in many cases. An enormous amount of prayer, love, and work is then spent persuading couples living out of wedlock to get married and join the church. It will take *concerted action* to break Pattern II.

This whole subject is of vital concern to the Churches. The masses cannot expect vigorous Christian life as long as most of their young people slide down into the Dark River and many never come up. The small classes cannot either, as long as they continue conditions which allow or encourage the Dark River to flow.

Jamaica has great achievements in public health, co-operative credit, education, communication and increased production. Despite these, stalwart character, basic integrity, and inbred reliability are not likely to be the lot of the 70 per cent of the population born out of wedlock and reared in the insecurity, hate, jealousy, intrigue and want which is built into Pattern II. Nor can that small proportion of the population which lives in Christian marriage from the beginning feel secure, for if relatives in Pattern II come to visit and servant girls with whom children are left practice Pattern II, it will cast its deadly shadows over the best homes. No one lives or dies to himself. The only way Christians can protect the way of life they cherish is to make it available to all. The only way the classes can achieve maximum morality is to lift the masses to a high level.

The best way in which the churches can grow significantly larger is to press forward on all three fronts, *creating Households of God free of Pattern II.* Our churches will grow both more soundly and more greatly in this Protestant Land when we *establish congregations which practice Christian marriage and pass it on to their children as a most precious possession.* This is one point at which Christians must dare to be different from the world.

We ponder the rapid increase of secularism and relativism with their loose moral standards in America and Europe, the baleful shadow of communism spreading insidiously all over the world, the probable increase in Moslem missionary activity which, allowing easy divorce, will ridicule Christian marriage as a thraldom unsuited to virile men anywhere, the Ras Tafari movement which some day may legalize Pattern II, and the declining influence of Christian ministers as "great men" in their communities. Possibly the *time left* in which Christians can establish Christian marriage as the Jamaican pattern may be shorter than we like to think.

CHAPTER V

CHURCH GROWTH, COMITY AND CO-OPERATION

The problem facing Churches in this island is *how to grow* when most Jamaicans belong, in a vague way, to some Church and yet three out of four adults are practicing Christians in none. The question is: Should a Church and its congregations seek to win the unchurched multitudes who regard themselves as in some way Christian?

Should *we* expand? Is the mounting multitude of the unchurched our business? In lands of many denominations, in these days of ecumenical conscience, these two questions face every Church. Whatever answers may be worked out on the co-operative level, each Church has its own answer to give. It dare not substitute "union efforts" or "good works" for *finding* lost sheep. It has an account to give to the Great Shepherd.

Each Church around the world should be committed to co-operation and—often—church union. Each should avoid anything approaching unbrotherly competition. It should prefer co-operative planning of church growth to launching out on its own. It should—in Jamaica— long for a union effort which would see the task of disciplining Jamaica as a whole, continuously chart unchurched areas, assign to each Church its sphere of work, and through adequate supervision proceed to a total disciplining of these hills and valleys.

However, despite the island-wide evangelistic campaign of a few years ago and considerable friendliness and co-operation between the Churches, especially the five now in union conversations, there has been no concerted charting of the opportunities and responsibilities for church growth, no month-by-month follow-up in each congregation, and no common course of instruction for converts. The leaders of the Churches do not give the time and energy which vigorous, co-operative evangelism of the thousand hill-and-valley, suburb-and-slum communities would require. Some Churches appear content with non-growing upper class membership and indisposed to make the radical changes which effective evangelism of the masses would require.

Thus each Church must either go forward, in utter friendliness but alone, enlarging its membership and planning new churches, or sit back longing and working for a united Church, watching opportunities for church growth disappear.

The only Church into which it can bring converts is its own. The nature of conversion is such that churches are able to win men and women into their own fellowships only. They cannot win them into other churches. Each Church in Jamaica should resolve, therefore, while welcoming any degree of co-operation, to forge ahead increasing its membership and multiplying its churches, as it finds unsaved men and women. Its sister Churches should do the same. Ardent evangelism should go hand in hand with ecumenical relations with all neighbors, frequent interchange of pulpits, and union services. No Church should seek anyone who is a practicing Christian in another Church, but it should seek all who are not.

Such a policy will lead any Church to competition with the old-line Churches, and also with the new-line

Churches of which the Churches of God are the best example. Jamaica is full of congregations of several branches of the Churches of God. They meet in bamboo-walled little churches 12 by 25 feet in dimension, or concrete-walled churches 16 by 40 feet. They are close neighbors of older churches everywhere. Their doctrines are soundly biblical. They are simple, devout, back-to-the-New-Testament churches of the common people. They are often ill-pastored, mount to a membership of 30 to 60 and stick there.

The Churches of God are churches of the masses. When slightly literate laborers become Christians in self-governing, self-supporting, and self-propagating churches, they will (no matter what their denomination) look like these Churches of God. Abundant proof of this can be found in the country congregations of the Anglicans, Presbyterians, Disciples of Christ, Methodists, and others in India, Latin America, Africa, Puerto Rico, and the Philippines. Most of these are less cultured, poorer, and meet in ruder church buildings than the Jamaican Churches of God. No self-supporting congregation of the masses, where the average education of the members is third standard or less, will conduct itself like Duke Street Christian Church or St. Paul's Presbyterian in Kingston. If it has spontaneous, natural Christian life, its members will talk and act like little-educated peasants and workmen do.

As old-line Christian Churches seek to be truly ecumenical, and at the same time to bring the unsaved into redemptive relationship to Jesus Christ our Lord, how should they treat the aggressive, converting, multiplying Churches of God? Two attitudes are possible: one a war to the finish; two, a resolve that even when they draw a circle to keep us out, we shall draw a circle to take them in. Nothing is to be gained by a war, except to delight Satan and his hosts. Cordial co-operation, scrupulous regard for their active membership, a willingness to learn from them the secret of their way with the masses, and a confidence that they are fundamentally as Christian as we, these things are pleasing to God.

Arrangements of expediency with old-line and new-line Churches, which will promote efficient building up of the Body of Christ and prevent overlapping and waste, are highly desirable. Often these arrangements can be made; but made or not, every church of Jesus Christ should persuade the four out of five adults who are not practicing Christians anywhere to become His followers. To preach a gospel pertinent to their lives, build congregations which enfold them in a satisfying fellowship, create churches which win them to natural life in God *at their present level* —this is the task. Co-operation or not, this must be done.

I. Church Growth and Nominality.

The question of whether Jamaica is over-churched runs headlong into a discussion of nominality. Each Church seeks to be surrounded by a community more or less affiliated to it. Members of this community are cordial to the church. They contribute to its rallies (public solicitations). They regard it as "our church." Though they may be living in Act One or Two, they count themselves Baptists, Friends, Anglicans or Methodists. They seldom attend worship or read the Bible. They may come to church for weddings or funerals or other special occasions. They do not personally know the power of God in their lives. They are not converted persons. They are nominal Christians.

Should they be counted as churched or unchurched? Due to their very large numbers, the question is central. Were this a Roman Catholic country, Evangelicals would without hesitation declare that these are unchurched people and leading them to Christ is in no sense sheep stealing. It is doing Christ's work of finding lost sheep. In America many ministers approach new people with the question "In what church are you working", and, if they are not *working* in any, count them unchurched. This would be good practice in Jamaica, or elsewhere in the world where nominal Christians are many in number.

II. "Divisive Competing Sects."

In this island from the beginning every effort to seek lost sheep and bring them to Christ has been vigorously opposed by the existing Churches on the ground that "Jamaica is plagued by troublesome divisive sects who confuse and mislead the people."

When in the first decades of the nineteenth century the Church of England was The Church in Jamaica— and numbered a few thousand whites in the midst of 400,000 pagan slaves,—it inveighed strenuously against the "intruding Methodists and Baptists."

In 1815 the Jamaica Assembly passed a resolution "carefully to investigate the means of diffusing the light of genuine Christianity (i.e., that of the Church of England) divested of the dark and dangerous fanaticism of the Methodists, which grafted on the African superstitions and working in the uninstructed minds and ardent temperament of the negroes, has produced the most pernicious consequences to individuals and is pregnant with imminent danger to the community." In 1828 the Assembly heard a report of its Committee on Sectarians which said of the Methodists and Baptists "that in order to extort money from their congregations and gain ascendancy over the negro mind, they inculcate the doctrines of equality and the rights of man;......and the consequences have been poverty, loss of comfort, and discontent among the slaves frequenting their chapels."

Philip Curtin, in *The Two Jamaicas* on page 70, says that in 1830 the Reverend George Bridges, an Anglican, claimed that "Christian sects (i.e., Methodists and Baptists) confuse the slaves and slow down the work of Christianization." But, continues Curtin, Bridges' sincerity is questionable since he took very little interest in Christianizing slaves! He wrote when the Church of England fee for administering the sacrament of baptism to a slave was a prohibitive one pound, three shillings and nine pence!

Baptists and Methodists (more the former than the latter) were persecuted, whipped, cast into jail, ridiculed, and libelled in the public press, as schismatic sectarians. The existing Church, despite the fact that it cared little for the effective Christianization of the population and was doing less, vigorously denounced those who did attempt effective evangelization.

Between 1850 and 1950 lines were drawn between the Churches, different strata of the population had gotten into each Church, and a *modus vivendi* had been established. There was much to do and general good feeling between those doing it. Each Church settled down to caring for its own. In an exploding population, co-operation increased while church membership remained stationary. Non-communicants increased from 340,000 to 1,200,000.

After World War I North American Churches, seeing the vast numbers of the unchurched, started sending missionaries to Jamaica. The American Branch of the Church of Rome intrenched itself solidly across the island behind parochial schools and carefully located churches. The small wealthy Chinese population of Kingston went largely Roman Catholic. The Churches of God found widespread responsiveness and established many small congregations throughout the hills. The Adventists were slower getting started but built for tomorrow with a wonderful training college at Mandeville and a strict discipline. They are a solid and rapidly growing Church. The Brethren, led by earnest spirit-filled men from the upper classes, rebelled against the lax standards of some of the old-line churches. Pattern II, gambling, drinking, and evangelistic torpidity forced them (they say) into the extension of their own stricter churches.

Thus today again, when only eight out of each hundred of the population are communicant members in the Anglican, Baptist, Moravian, Presbyterian, Congregational, and Christian Churches; and when Churches of God, Assemblies of God, Seventh Day Adventists, United Brethren, Pilgrim Holiness, and others attempt effective evangelization of the unchurched masses, a chorus of protests arises from at least some of the old-line Churches that these "divisive sectarian efforts" confuse the people and must at all costs be stopped. Whether such protests are pleasing to God should be carefully pondered.

As in the early 1800's the Church of England and the Presbyterian Church, being Churches of the slave owners, debarred themselves from effective Christianization of the slaves, so today the old-line Churches, having become largely upper class, have weakened themselves for the Christianization of the masses. Just as the Church of England ought to have welcomed the incoming Methodists and Baptists, but did not; so old-line Churches today should welcome the incoming Churches of the people, but find it difficult to do so. Always, of course, on impeccable theological and ecclesiastical grounds!

True, these "young-line" Churches—often arrogantly called sects—ought to take some of the blame for not getting on with the old-line Churches. They are often so condemnatory of the old-line Churches, so sure they are right, and so blithely overlook the deeply consecrated Christians among us and the scars of battle we bear. They so easily form exclusive associations. They so often take our less loyal members. In 1942 Dr. Merle Davis of the International Missionary Council, an impartial outsider, wrote very strongly against what he calls "sectarian confusion".

Granting all this, the fact remains that out of this "confusion" has come *the only church growth this century has seen*. There are about 100,000 communicant Christians in these new Branches of the Church of Christ. Would these be members of the old-line Churches if the new Branches had not come in? Not likely. On the contrary, there is some evidence that the new-line Churches have galvanized the old-line to renewed efforts.

Herein lies the dilemma. This "confusion", this "ugly division", is *disciplining the masses*. The old-line Churches are not. What should they do?

The old-line Churches would do well both to surge

forward bringing to active commitment the nominal Christians found in such numbers and to welcome all Branches of the Church, even those on the left and right who feel so separate and righteous. Neither evangelization by itself nor co-operation by itself is the answer. As much co-operation and union as can be obtained *while multiplying evangelism* is required. Stopping evangelization to push 'church union' is fatal. It is highly doubtful whether a union of stopped Churches will suddenly find itself concerned about the unchurched and able to confer on them the gift of the Holy Spirit.

Appeals on the grounds of comity and co-operation to other bodies not to enter the Jamaican field will, in this highly competitive era, restrain those Evangelicals closest to the old-line Churches, are not likely to restrain the most distant Evangelicals, and will certainly not restrain the Romans. The best procedure is not, then, to bewail competition but to bring multitudes of the unchurched living at our very gates into vital life giving relationship to Jesus Christ. As long as we permit eight hundred thousand adults to remain out of Christ, we have no grounds to complain if other Churches find and add these lost sheep.

III. The Bearing on Mission in Other Lands

Few lands of Africasia have the problems of comity and co-operation faced by Jamaica.

In over ninety per cent of non-Christian populations, cordial good will and common sense, coupled with whole countrysides which had never heard the Gospel, have brought it about that in any given town or district only one Branch of the Church of Christ is at work.

Yet perhaps ten per cent of missions work in big cities and lands easy to enter and pleasant to live in. There comity and co-operation pose much the same problems as in Jamaica—several static Churches 'hold' the field, unchurched multitudes mount, and a cry goes up against anyone else coming in.

Often churches can multiply and movements to Christ can mature, but do not, because the old-line Churches and missions have learned patiently to come out of unripe fields empty handed. When fields ripen, they still come out empty handed. When men can be won, the Churches and missions are tied up in education, medicine, literacy or some non-reproductive form of "evangelism". They have been ploughing so long, they have forgotten to harvest.

In this small but important section of its total field, world mission should ask itself some questions. What should world mission do with those missions and Churches which for various reasons are busy on the side lines, serenely watching the population explode? In the light of Jamaica, what attitude should intrenched Churches have to new arrivals? Should world mission guarantee existing Churches complete monopoly? And do the correct answers to these questions depend on the degree to which the Churches are *in fact* carrying out the Great Commission?

In answering these questions several principles may be borne in mind. First, while co-operation is good, it is not enough. Most missions and Churches in Africasia already work together to make the best use of existing resources. Such co-operation among little-growing Churches and their supporting missions is, however, no answer to the unchurched multitudes.

Second, mergers of Churches are good, but not enough. They are happening neither fast enough nor completely enough. When all which now seem remotely possible have happened, we shall still have many Churches both of the Catholic right and the Christian left which carry on mission outside the merged Churches. Furthermore, to date, many united Churches are relatively static. Thus in Puerto Rico between 1940 and 1955 while seven other Branches of the Church of Christ (Baptist, Methodist, etc.) were showing considerable growth, the United Church Branch was showing no growth at all.

While co-operation and union have great values, Christians must ask themselves this question: is it well to prevent any other seeking of the lost except that which the existing Church of a given district chooses to do? Are there good grounds for believing that under the impact of the world mission, upper class Churches will remould themselves so that they search for and appeal to the unchurched masses? Or that lower class Churches will so change as to win the upper classes? Does evidence indicate that sleeping Churches, when undisturbed by troublesome neighbors, rouse and become greatly growing Churches? Should the unity of the Church, for which we all pray, be such as gives intrenched Churches undisputed occupation of their fields so that unbelievers will not be confused with varying versions of the Good News? Or will this rather make the intrenched Churches sleep all the more soundly? These are life and death questions for millions of nominal Christians and uncounted multitudes of non-Christians who have become responsive to the Gospel.

Third, awesome necessity requires that all messengers

of Christ, whether they be of Cephas, Apollos, Paul, or
Silas be welcomed. The task is too big and the days too
urgent for any attempt to keep Christ's people out of white
harvest fields. Static Churches growing at a mere 15 to
20 per cent a decade have urgent need for assistance—
whether they want it or not. They need the stimulus
which comes from seeing others bring in sheaves.

The Church of Christ again faces the situation described in Mark 9. "John said, 'Teacher we saw a man
casting out demons in your name and we forbade him,
because he was not following us'. But Jesus said, 'Do not
forbid him; for no one who does a mighty work in my
name will be able soon after to speak evil of me. For he
that is not against us is for us." Facing the stupendous
harvest fields of today, Churches should pray the Lord
to send forth reapers, and also gladly welcome all He
sends.

Losses, to be sure, occur through a divided witness—
and all Christians, repenting of denominationalism, should
seek a spirit of harmony and unity. Yet losses occasioned
by static Churches and lack of reapers are much greater.
Ah, the ripened grain which will soon fall down and rot!
Ah, the masses living without Christ and dying in great
thirst never having access to the Living Water!

Fourth, religious liberty also requires an open door.
In the coming great debate between the religions of man-
kind, the one inflexible rule must be freedom of conscience.
Truth is invincible. The Christian asks for himself free-
dom to proclaim Christ. He must grant to other Christians
a similar freedom. The enemy is not competition.
The great enemy is an arrangement between existing
Churches (or it may be religions) to stifle free proclamation

and leave men chained to nominal—and largely lifeless—
adherence to ancestral religion.

Fifth, pastoral responsibility also demands the maximum finding of lost sheep. If little-growing Churches or
their Councils frown on or prevent other Churches or missions from coming in, will they be responsible for the souls
of men who through the new comers might have believed
in Christ? Will they be responsible for the Word which
was not proclaimed? Dare a good shepherd refuse help
when the lost sheep are so numerous he cannot feed and
fold them? Or when he has become so feeble or "busy",
that he can no longer search for them?

Sixth, different populations demand different dealing.
Common sense has led and should lead most Christian
bodies to leave each population of little response to one
Church and mission. But in populations where a vast
thirst exists beyond the power or inclination of the existing
Churches to quench, additional Churches should be
urgently invited to come in. Between the irresponsive and
the highly responsive lie many populations. In them
study is needed of what procedures in these racing days
best revive and expand the Church of Christ and all its
Branches.

IV. Preying On Another Flock?

Where the existing Church is growing satisfactorily
and some other Church comes in to make disciples not of
'the world' but of already active members t,here none of
the principles heretofore annunciated apply. There,
the New Testament practice of opposing Cephas "to his
face," and presenting the right as God gives us to see the

right, but within the spirit of Christ, is required. Conflict is inescapable in life.

With fantastic numbers of men and women living without either knowledge of Christ or participation in Him, persuading active Methodists to become Lutherans or active Baptists to become Adventists is inexcusable.

In summary, in Jamaica and around the world, each Church should multiply disciples and churches greatly, out to the limit of the available population,—with as much co-operation and unity as it is possible to obtain.

CHAPTER VI

A TYPICAL CHURCH STRUCTURE

Church growth never happens "in general". It always means the increase of a specific Church or, more exactly, of specific congregations. The rate of growth is never uniform among Churches and congregations. Some grow more, some less, and some stand still or shrink.

Hence to understand church growth in Jamaica, it is necessary to see some one Church in considerable detail and to ponder what growth will mean in its congregations. Complete understanding of the Church in Jamaica would require seeing each Church and its congregations.

But reading of the structures of a dozen Churches, all somewhat similar, arising out of similar background, and facing the same problems is weary work. Hence this book presents the structure of only one—the Christian Church (Disciples of Christ), which we shall hereafter call simply "The Christian Church." Perhaps its catholic name will enable kindly readers to see it as representative of the larger stronger Churches of the Island.

True, the Baptist, Anglican, Presbyterian, Methodist and Moravian Churches have more and larger congregations. Their members include a much larger proportion of upper class people and a much smaller proportion of people of the masses. They have more wealth, culture, and education than the Christian Church. Their members play a much larger part in society, government, industry, and education.

Notwithstanding these differences, the Christian Church in this island is a true Jamaican Church. All other Churches here resemble it much more than they do a Church in Oregon, England, or Tanganyika. Church growth in Jamaica means the growth of congregations (of whatever denomination) like those described in the following pages. Hence we trust the Christian Church will serve as a useful medium of understanding.

We have pointed out the lowly status of the Christian Church and the differences between it and the other old-line Churches. Because of these differences, the other Churches will find more, not less, difficulty in growing from the masses—and the unchurched masses are the only segments of society in which great growth can occur. The task of church growth, seen in the light of the structure of the Christian Church, will look easier than it really is for the other old-line Churches.

I. **The Tabular Picture**

Let us look, first of all, at the groupings, location, and memberships of the congregations of the Christian Church.

According to number of circuits, the Christian Church is rural 10 to 1. According to number of congregations, it is rural 30 to 5. According to number of members, it is rural only 27 to 15. The rural membership lives, not in villages, but in homes scattered over the hillsides, each house on its own land, be that a quarter acre or ten. Very few members live within a hundred yards of the church building. Many walk one or two miles through very hilly country to worship there.

The rural churches are grouped in ten circuits with an educated minister living in a good parsonage in the "center" of the circuit.   Thus each minister has about 250 members who contribute about two hundred pounds ($600) a year to his salary.   Two circuits—Olivet and Zion —lie a few miles due east of Kingston along the south coast, in the mountains rising from it, and form a compact unit 5 by 9 miles in extent.   Three circuits—Chepstowe, Caenwood, and Craigmill—are on the north side of the island across the 7,000 feet Blue Mountain Ridge.   Five circuits—Mannings Hill, Mt. Industry, Oberlin, Providence, and High Gate—lie in the hills in a line which stretches across the island north northwest from Kingston.

The town and city churches are five in number. Each of the three strong churches in Kingston has a a minister of its own. In addition, there is one mission church at Pretoria Road. High Gate is a strong, well-led church in a small town on the north side of the Island. Since there is no Baptist Church in High Gate, by what historic accident I do not know, the Christian Church gets all Christians who hold to believers' baptism. Leaders in High Gate include some upper class people, though the great bulk of the members are humble folk-—many of them farmers, peasants, and laborers.

With headquarters in the city of Kingston, close connections with the upper class Churches in the seminary, large congregations in Torrington, Duke Street, and Kings Gate, and things happening in the city of Kingston all the time to attract the car-equipped ministers, there is a tendency for the country people to be neglected and for patterns of action to be laid down suitable to the Kingston churches but impractical in the small towns and the hills. For the hill churches to thrive, this built-in bias toward urban work will have to be recognized and resisted.

The Tabular Picture of Church Structure

Circuit	Church	Minister	Membership 1956	Membership 1957	Exam	CYF	CWF	CMF	SS	Total Giving in pounds
1. High Gate	1. Seaton	Morris	34	43	...	30	...	...	30	28
	2. Mt. Vernon	...	89	95	90	...	...	...	35	42
	3. Airy Mt.	...	36	34	...	13	...	...	27	14
2. Providence	4. Providence	Goldson	114	128	82	...	...	...	57	89
	5. Flint River	...	69	88	...	...	...	...	57	43
	6. Chesterfield	...	155	160	...	...	...	...	55	70
3. Caenwood	7. Caenwood	Seaton	86	108	...	...	...	...	...	48
	8. Mt. Gracious	...	143	148	...	64	...	...	75	89
	9. Commodore	...	83	105	...	...	...	...	...	33
4. Chepstowe	10. Chepstowe	Metz	78	87	...	20	13	...	61	43
	11. Fairy Hill	...	25	31	...	...	...	...	...	43
	12. Ythanside	...	15	15	...	...	...	...	...	...
5. Craigmill	13. Craigmill	Millard	128	144	...	...	30	...	52	110
	14. Berea	...	65	70	...	...	...	...	67	49
6. Mannings Hill	15. Mannings Hill	Townsend	92	90	104	20	30	...	72	113
	16. Salisbury Plains	...	79	85	75	15	20	...	41	37

Circuit	No.	Church									
7. Mt. Industry	17.	Mt. Industry	Dunkley	254	265	...	72	60	...	324	236
	18.	London Ridge	...	78	79	75	...	...	...	53	67
	19.	Lucky Hill	...	110	110	...	...	...	...	...	57
	20.	Williamsfield	...	27	32	...	...	...	...	31	37
8. Mt. Olivet	21.	Mt. Olivet	Hart	57	72	61	...	...	...	40	91
	22.	Bloxburgh	...	140	124	94	...	...	...	70	100
	23.	New Bethel	...	76	77	68	...	...	...	30	82
	24.	Friendship Brook	...	75	76	...	...	...	...	20	29
	25.	Mt. Carmel	...	27	27	...	...	...	...	20	76
9. Mt. Zion	26.	Mt. Zion	Nelson	76	85	79	33	...	...	86	66
	27.	Bushy Park	...	83	93	...	20	...	...	42	151
	28.	New Bethlehem	...	34	37	29	...	10	...	60	54
	29.	Manheim	...	...	20	24	24	...	...	...	6
10. Oberlin Circuit	30.	Oberlin	Robertson	152	186	154	30	20	...	139	139
Totals for country churches				2518	2748	...	...	...	...	...	2032
1. Town and City Churches	1.	High Gate	Morris	238	242	...	30	...	...	80	342
	2.	Pretoria Road	Metz	88	96	74	24	25	9	50	127
	3.	King's Gate	Redding	250	286	...	24	30	18	80	828
	4.	Duke Street	Horber	433	509	...	55	50	15	259	777
	5.	Torrington	Edwards	391	454	...	40	40	17	200	1041
Totals for City Churches				1400	1587	...	...	...	...	...	3115
Grand Totals				3918	4835	...	...	...	...	...	5147

II. **Membership**

Turning to the membership columns, we see that in 1957 the total reported for the country churches was 2748 and for the city 1587.   The 1956 figures are 2518 and 1400. If we let our eye run up and down these columns we see a lift in membership in most cases.

If, however, we look at the column headed "Exam," we find generally lower figures.   These "Exam" column figures are what we found as we went through the rolls, making age and status analyses.   When the elder, the church secretary, a few members, and we went through the roll making an estimate of the age of each member and his married or single status, we came up with 17 per cent less members in 12 churches chosen at random than had been reported seven months before.

This underscores the continuing need, in any program of church expansion, in any land, of putting a firm foundation of fact under church strategy.   Statistics which are 17 per cent off give an impression of growth which is not there.   I was unable to check the larger city memberships.   The machinery simply does not exist for an accurate accounting of it and there are indications that the memberships reported are approximations.   For example, Duke Street with a membership of 509 reported that it lost in 1957 only two members, which seems unlikely in a big city church with many members coming and going. Records of baptisms in all churches were too incomplete to include in this report at all.

Printed forms, including definitions and examples of who is a member, are essential to accuracy.   So is regular painstaking examination of the roll by the ministers and the field secretary. Only then can reliance be placed on the statistics.

The thirty hillside churches fall into three groups: eight *little* churches of from 15 to 43 members; seventeen *small* churches of from 70 to 110 members; and five *larger* churches from 144 to 265 in membership. The "little" ones—with one exception, Fairy Hill—should be considered branch churches.   Of the five "larger" churches, only two really deserve to be so called—Oberlin because of the high school and Mt. Industry with its huge elementary school. The others— Chesterfield, Craigmill, and Mt. Gracious—are very like the small churches, except they happen to have a somewhat larger membership. With the right kind of shepherding, most of the "small" churches could grow to 150 members; and, without it, these "larger" churches would rapidly diminish to less than 100, as Bloxburgh has.

The age of the members is important. The long, thin age distribution given in the picture of the Dark River is that which, with minor variations, obtains in rural churches. It would be well to turn back to the picture in Chapter IV and ponder both the age distribution of the communicants and the large numbers of people, living within two miles but *not in these or any other churches*.

Teenagers and adults of the 20 to 39 year grouping form a minute part of the membership. The hills hold very great numbers of them. Only a small part—possibly a quarter—goes to the city or emigrates. *They are there in the small towns and the hills*. But they do not form part of the church. They are actively out of the churches

III. **Auxiliary Organizations**

The eleven Christian Youth Fellowships (CYF)

reported from the hillside churches should be understood as bands of about half a dozen young people each who meet weekly in a little service led by a fine young woman in a brave attempt to "meet the needs of youth".

When they get good adult leadership, the program is somewhat more varied and nourishing. CYF'ers seldom if ever engage in any kind of witness work, house-to-house teaching, evangelism, tract distribution, or outside Sunday School work. Prior to 1956 very few of them were members of the Church. In the drive for members last year a good number of them have been baptized and are now communicants.

Notwithstanding the difficulties, however, youth work —x, y, and z see page 55—needs to be pushed in every church, on both the "accept Christ and wait chastely for a long while before getting married" basis and the "accept Christ and get married early" basis. There will be heavy losses on the first basis, but some z youth will remain faithful and x and y youth, while small in number, are among the future leaders of this land. If early marriage becomes common, z youth will be the mainstay of the rural churches.

The Sunday Schools, judged by American standards, are in poor condition. Yet considering the total situation, they represent considerable victory. They usually have four classes: Beginners, Primaries, Juniors, Intermediates; and sometimes a fifth—Adults. The enrollments of 20 to 70 means average attendances of 10 to 30—i.e., four or five little classes of 3 to 10 pupils each. Weekly meetings for training teachers are rare. We found no instances. The teachers teach the materials put into their hands after they arrive. Where the day school teachers are earnest

Christians—as in the nine teacher schools held in the churches at Mt. Industry and Oberlin—a much higher standard of teaching and attendance is achieved. Other notable Sunday Schools are those at Torrington and Duke Street.

In most cases, the Sunday Schools do not lead into the Church. Except for x and y sections of this population (perhaps 100 youth in all these churches—or an average of 3 to a church) the Sunday School ends around 12-14 and the Dark River begins.[1] Nevertheless, it is well to push on with the Sunday School. In the years ahead the Churches and the State are going to end the Dark River as a recognized Jamaican institution. Even if this is half accomplished, the Sunday School will give greater yields in the future than it has in the past. Then, too, those who have had Sunday School teaching in their youth are more likely to come out of the Dark River than those who have had none.

The Christian Women's Fellowships (CWF) and the Christian Men's Fellowships (CMF) in the rural churches are not doing well. Seven rural churches have organizations called CWFs, but there is little evidence of fruitful meetings. They are rather like Saul's armour and tend to become—with inadequate leadership—"another organization" to institute. The basic goals of these organizations could be achieved if the Sunday School were to have a women's class and a men's class with lessons geared to

(1) Another pattern prevails among upper class members of upper class Churches. Their children are x youth, among whom a vigorous Christian education will lead to profession of faith in Christ and thus to confirmation or baptism. The pattern of the Christian Church prevails in upper class Churches, however, among members from the masses. Their youth also are z youth. For these the Sunday School ends at 12-14 and the Dark River begins.

the *actual conditions and needs of the hillside people*. Successful classes could then hold mid-week sessions as their program grew to demand it.

In the city churches, on the other hand, both CYF and CWF are doing well, serve a useful function, and should be vigorously promoted.

The adult section of the Sunday School is of great importance. Without it, adolescents do not stay on to Sunday School. With adults studying God's Word regularly as a matter of joy and duty, when John and Mary get big enough to assert their independence, they will be more likely to do like the "big people" do—come to Sunday School. Furthermore, adults need Bible study. Since the church membership is so elderly, the Church School should enroll many elderly people.

IV. **The Support of the Church—Tithes and Offerings**

The "total giving" column of the Tabular Picture is full of hope. To begin with, it is not the total giving of the church. It is what is reported to the Central Committee of the Christian Church. All churches give more than this. Some give twice this. They do not always spend wisely—for example, one church was paying an organist five pounds a month which was more than half what it gave to the Association Program through the Central Committee. A good deal of the work of even poor churches, that should be volunteer, is paid for.

If what is paid into the Central Committee were doubled, the ministry would be entirely self-supporting. This goal can be readily achieved. Jamaicans of the masses are not poor in comparison with rural Filipinos,

Orissans, Congolese, and others. Compared with them, they eat well and live well. The present giving to the Central Committee is less than four pence per member per week for the rural churches and less than six pence for the urban ones. This can be easily doubled. Indeed, the Christian Church should aim to quadruple it.

There has been some pressure for increased giving. When suitably applied, it has brought good results. But much more teaching of the Biblical system of giving is needed. Simple effective tracts on tithing are lacking. "The tithe is the Lord's" is not being taught. In the absence of such teaching, talk about the tithe tends to sound like a device to squeeze more money out of a reluctant people.

A dozen lessons on "Tithes and Offerings: What the Bible Says" used in the Sunday Schools for a solid quarter every second year would help rectify the situation. Outlines of sermons on tithes and offerings sent out to each minister on subsidized salary to be used once a quarter would help. Teams of laymen, themselves tithers, could visit each church and teach their fellows. Only ministers who tithe into the church treasury should be ordained and employed.

"We are poor people and cannot give" needs to be replaced by "We poor people cannot afford to loose God's blessing through robbing Him and impoverishing our churches." Nothing can replace conviction based on the Bible.

V. Occupation, Education, and Buildings

Occupation. Both the men and the much more numerous women of the hillside churches fall roughly into three groupings: (1) a few 5 to 25 acre persons, who never hire themselves out as labor and who often employ others; (2) some 1 to 4 acre persons who rent other land also and do most of their own work, and who seldom hire themselves out; and (3) some landless persons, or very small landholders who regularly hire themselves out and are always the servants of others. Some members keep a little store, do tailoring, carpentry, or mason work.

Well-to-do peasants (5 to 25 acre persons) keep cattle, mules, and borrow money from the banks for various productive purposes. They live in comfortable houses with solid walls, good furniture, tight roofs, and big barbeques (solid pavements used as drying floors).

Increasingly, even on the hillsides, water is being piped into the houses. Where it is not, peasants catch water off the roofs or carry it from a spring.

In seven country churches the Christian Church runs schools. In five cases these are conducted in the church building. In these seven congregations, the teachers are also members. In times past, teachers regarded themselves as part of the church, were dependent for employment on the minister who was also school manager, and were helpful in the church and Sunday School. Where they were in addition devout, convinced Christians, they were a tremendous blessing to the church. Today, schools are becoming increasingly secular, teachers do not feel dependent on the minister-manager, and the Christian Church gets chiefly teachers of other denominations. Consequently in some cases teachers are no help to the church. In some, notably at Mt. Industry, they are the life of the church. Where the teacher is a member, she is usually church secretary and the books are well kept.

In the city, Christian Church members are largely servant girls, laborers, artizans, factory workers, and vegetable growers from the edge of Kingston. But together with these are some middle class persons—contractors, clerks, teachers, school principals, insurance agents, car salesmen, and the like.

Education. In the country congregations, a portion of the members are illiterate, another portion barely literate, and still another portion read and write with ease. Since into the church, via the marriage route, are taken only the more successful of the peasantry, the level of literacy in the churches is above that in the countryside. What is the rate of literacy? If it means ability to read the Bible with ease, then less than 50 per cent are literate. If it means ability to sign one's own name only, then about 80 per cent are literate. As we listened to the Bible being read in Sunday School classes and women's meetings (which enroll the more dedicated and able among the membership), we were impressed by the number who read hesitantly.

Only a small part of the membership is sixth pass or equivalent. Those passing the sixth have, for the most part, gone on to various forms of training, have moved to the city, or have emigrated.

In the city, on the other hand, each congregation has a sizable section of educated men and women—not many high school and college graduates, but persons who have grown since leaving school. They read the daily papers and work with figures and facts in offices and other places of employment. Incidentally the churches might well emphasize post-school, adult education.

Buildings. The Christian Churches in Jamaica

have many beautiful, adequate and permanent buildings.

Some stone churches are stately buildings on hills and date back many years. Some have been built since 1952 and are largely of reinforced concrete.

The pews, organs, pianos, pulpits, and choir lofts are good. Seven of the ten circuits have manses.

The town churches have large sanctuaries. Even the little "mission" church in Pretoria Road has a big new sanctuary which—if the membership trebles—will become the hall or church school plant. Most buildings would house congregations twice as big as now exist.

VI. **Mission Aid**

In a day when hundreds of millions are being spent annually by older Churches (East and West) for the aid of younger Churches, one must ask "What aid has this Church received from its assisting mission and how has this influenced church growth"

As shown in the following graph, large amounts of American aid have been used between 1942 and 1955 without the church growing at all. Missionary and current expense costs multiplied ten times while membership stood still.

In 1955 the membership stood at 3,252. In the next two years it climbed to 4,335 and then stood at close to that figure for the next two years, being only 4,394 in 1959. The eleven hundred increase includes (a) paper gains made by a new definition of members, (b) seventeen per cent over estimation of members, and (c) a considerable number of adolescents whose chances of "falling away" are very good.

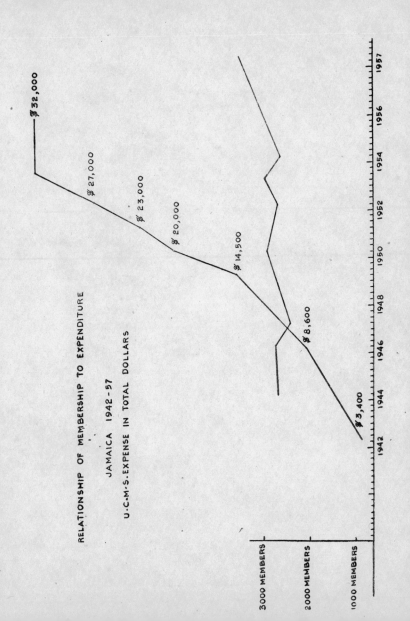

RELATIONSHIP OF MEMBERSHIP TO EXPENDITURE

JAMAICA 1942-57

U·C·M·S·EXPENSE IN TOTAL DOLLARS

$32,000

$27,000

$23,000

$20,000

$14,500

$8,600

$3,400

3000 MEMBERS

2000 MEMBERS

1000 MEMBERS

1942 1944 1946 1948 1950 1952 1954 1956 1957

Shall we say that in 1955 the large amounts of mission aid began to affect membership favorably? We do not think so, though the answer is correct to this extent—generous mission aid during the preceding twelve years had created a feeling of well-being. Churches had been rebuilt. Pastors salaries were subsidized and stabilized. A secondary school had been established. Missionaries had buttressed various aspects of church life.

But these things by themselves did not produce the upturn. That came when the attention of the Church was focussed by the assisting mission on the fifty year period of non-growth. A rising concern with impotence in mission was being felt. Leaders became increasingly loath to define mission as "aid in perpetuity to stopped little younger Churches". Great need was recognized for the younger Church to become more evidently the Body of Christ and more effective in finding lost persons. These deep movements of the spirit were finally expressed in a searching question. The mission asked "Shall we classify you as a static younger Church, unable to grow?" The Christian commitment of the Church replied, "Certainly not. We can and will grow".

It began to take seriously its duty and privilege to reconcile men to God. It renewed evangelistic effort. It concentrated attention on weak churches and was more concerned that families come out of the Dark River. It requested a study of church growth (of which this book is the outcome) to help it see the dimensions of the problem.

While the results were gratifying, the temporary nature of the upturn with a new plateau indicates that still deeper response and still greater communication of the Gospel is required.

VII. **The Crucial Task**.

For what does this—or any—church structure exist? Memberships, auxiliary organizations, tithes, church buildings, mission aid—what does God require of them? Certainly that of winning men to Christ is a chief one. With vast unchurched populations on every side, any Church not reconciling men to God is as dead as Lazarus and much less likely to be resurrected. Any genuine Church will engage in mission as of its very nature—and mission under Jamaican circumstances will mean at least persuading fellow citizens to become disciples of Christ and responsible members of His Church.

The task then is for these specific congregations— where they now are, weak as they now are, blessed as they now are—to bring converts into their fellowships for further worship of and obedience to God-in-Christ. We have looked carefully at the structure—not as an abstract intellectual exercise—but to estimate aright what church growth at this level, in this Church and these congregations must mean. Since church growth always depends on the nature of the population being evangelized, we now look at the rural and urban field separately.

Rural congregations in Jamaica have a remarkable advantage. They are composed of the most successful persons in the locality. Just because membership is so often tied up with respectability, and marriage with financial competence, those who have "arrived" tend to become members. Responsible, industrious, forceful people usually become Christians. To foreigners from across the sea or to educated Jamaicans the rural congregations may seem weak, yet they contain the leaders of the communities. The rural churches are in a strong position. Their members have both standing and intimate contact through social, business, and marriage relations with all the people of their neighborhoods.

When discussing church growth, leaders of the rural congregations often say that within a couple of miles of every Christian church are from three to ten other church-es. And this is true. Yet two considerations must be borne in mind. First, that many of these others are church-es of less than 40 members—struggling little bands of Christians, visited once a month (or once a quarter) by an ordained minister who lives in a central place and has a circuit of two to six little congregations. Second, that when all the memberships of the area are added up, a figure results which is a small part, perhaps one fifth, of the adult population. Four out of five of the adults in the valleys and hillsides immediately adjacent to Christ-ian churches are *out of any church whatever*. They will often have a church preference. They will take their babies to "their" church for christening. But they are commu-nicant members of no church and seldom worship, though they sometimes attend special functions. Thus on close inspection the "over-churched" nature of the Jamaican rural scene, often adduced as a sufficient reason for lack of church growth, disappears into thin air.

These rural multitudes pose a challenge. They pre-sent a great opportunity for church growth. They are friendly to the Church. They are basically Protestant people and as able potentially as men and women any-where. They can be won—as spurts of growth in days past indicate,—but they can be lost, too. At Fairy Hill decades ago, with a resident pastor, Reverend A. O. Aitcheson, in the pulpit and Miss Edna Harrison in the school, the membership, despite the Church of God a couple of hundred yards down the road, grew to 120. It is now down to 31. The country people can be won, but the program which will win them and hold them will be something more than what most Christian churches have now. It will be more natural, fervent, and biblical.

The urban field is even more hopeful and urgent than the rural. The city of Kingston, like cities everywhere, has grown enormously. It is in the midst of runaway suburban expansion. It is now five miles north and south and three miles east and west. Long Mountain to the east prevents expansion in that direction. But to the west lies a plain of about six square miles in extent all divided up into lots. Many of these are already sold and some builded upon. Roads have been laid out in much of it and a water system complete with red hydrants has been laid. By 1970 this entire plain will be full of houses.

The development of this huge area is in the hands of real estate companies who, subject to municipal regulations, divide it into lots put in roads and water, and sell at a profit. Some sections will become exclusive residential areas with houses costing ten to twenty thousand dollars. Others will become ordinary residential areas with houses costing two to five thousand dollars. In still other cases, government steps in and puts up four or five hundred houses for the poor. These cost about fifteen hundred dollars and sell on a twenty-year payment plan.

In 1958 we traversed this vast area block after block, mile after mile, development after development. Even in the built-up sections we saw very few churches, while in the plotted but unsold or unbuilt sections there were none. The Anglicans and the Roman Catholics have purchased at half price the few church lots provided by government in the low-price housing developments, but we saw only four new churches—one Presbyterian, one Congregational, one Roman Catholic, and one Assemblies of God. The Church Union Commission was offered a fine site some 18 months ago for 1,700 pounds. When it could not buy, the site was offered to the Roman Catholics, who immediately bought it.

In addition to the plain to the west, Kingston has the Mona Development to the northeast around the new University of the West Indies and several small developments here and there. Ewarton in the center of the island will see considerable urbanization in connection with the aluminium plant.

After seeing the rural opportunity quite extensively, driving considerable distances, climbing up to the hillside churches, meeting small congregations, and seeing the footwork involved in tramping the hillsides, the ease and availability of the urban opportunity strikes one with great force. Here within twenty minutes of the established Christian churches, on good paved roads, lie great new developments with no church in them at all. Enormous opportunity for planting churches exists.

Here they are—tens of thousands of the most winnable people in the world, conveniently congregated in a great modern city, on flat ground traversed by excellent roads. They are not Moslems, not Hindus, and not Communists. They are citizens of a State where the Church still has prestige. It would be quite possible for the Christian Church to plant and bring to maturity ten congregations of 200 to 500 members each in the next decade.

Yet it would not be easy. Building these urban masses into self-supporting, self-governing, and self-propagating churches will take special planning, consecration, footwork, sweat,—and tears. It cannot be done by pouring in money from abroad—to buy sites and put up churches. It must begin with the existing congregations. It must find some way of reaching the heart of the masses. It must fling bridges across the Dark River. It must train a ministerial leadership which knows how to bring men to penitence and to Christ. It must create a membership which knows and uses the kerygma and which fervently believes that accepting Jesus Christ as Saviour is a matter of eternal significance. The pressure to evangelize, the fire burning in the bones, the "woe is me if I preach not the Gospel" cannot be generated by any mission board in England or America—or it will be resented by Jamaicans! That pressure is a *sine qua non;* but it must well up in Jamaican hearts as they stand in the presence of the Saviour and the cross.

Given this Jamaican initiative, help from abroad can be used to the glory of God.

Defined pragmatically, mission today is the fine art of so combining the convictions and resources of older and younger Churches that great populations are claimed for Jesus Christ and, as recorded again and again in the book of Acts, "multitudes are added to the Lord."

Such is the structure of the Christian Church in Jamaica. God has created it for expansion in such a time as this. As Jamaica surges forward into new life, as it pushes education among its masses, as new measures of health, income, culture, and agricultural production become possible, these Christian churches stand on the edge of vast opportunities for expansion. Every congregation should double and most of them should treble their membership in the next decade. The structure is here. The buildings are here. The church boards, deacons, and elders are here. The Sunday Schools, Women's Fellowships, Men's Fellowships, mission aid, and even parochial schools are here. Few fields are so greatly blessed with the material, organizational appurtenances to growth.

The tide is coming in. As it comes, it will lift Christian people. The Church does not need to trouble itself about increased agricultural production, increased education, increased handicrafts, teaching people how to use galvanized iron sheets for roofing, and the like. It does not need to establish co-operative credit societies or chicken-raising establishments. These are being done by the State better than the churches can do them. All the churches need to do is to use the structure which they have inherited—the labor of devoted forebears—to multiply Christians inside existing churches and to multiply branch churches and new churches in vacant fields. This is the greatest service they can render to their neighbors, their island, and their Lord.

CHAPTER VII

MEANING FOR MISSION

This volume looks closely at Churches in Jamaica searching for their meanings for Christian Mission everywhere. Where are century long trends in mission leading us? Looking steadily at the end goal—that the world be reconciled to God in Christ—how far along is Christian Mission? What main obstacles are being met? What major emphases are needed?

Four main meanings emerge. They are not the only meanings—many more have been mentioned; but they dominate the scene like the snow-capped peaks of the Oregon mountains.

I.   The Main Stage of Mission Lies Ahead

When a population has been evangelized, when a country's leaders are largely church members, when those who become Christian are not persecuted, then the main stage of mission has begun. Many are still out of the churches. Many are nominal Christians. Many remain unwon because they belong to a different class, speak a different language, have a different sized income, or have customs the Church cannot condone. This remainder may be a large part of the general population as in Jamaica or a small part of one tribe or caste from which large numbers have become Christian. Remainders are often winnable. They are intimately connected with church members by social, business, and marriage relationships. They respect Christians. Nevertheless they remain out of the Church. Winning the remainder is the main stage of mission.

In the main stage the problem is not hostile nationalisms, rival religions, or furious persecution. The problem lies in other areas. Perhaps God has so elevated His people that they have lost contact with their own folk. Perhaps the Churches and their assisting missions have faced some great barrier for so long that they have despaired of surmounting it and have grown used to multitudes remaining on the other side. Perhaps Churches are lacking in vision, accustomed to being a minority, and too separated from the unsaved to be able to communicate the Gospel to them.

Is carrying out the main stage a responsibility of world mission? Or is it rightly that of the Churches of that land?

Let us, first, plead the case for national Churches assuming this responsibility. The huge task of world evangelization remains yet to do. Hence World Mission says to national Churches, "The first stage is completed. Like Paul, we must go elsewhere. Your task is to complete the evangelization. Furthermore you do not want us complicating your task, pointing out your errors, or even gently encouraging you to action. To ensure brotherly relations, we must leave. The Lord bless and empower you." From many points of view this seems to be a right decision.

Yet what happens when, on taking such a stand, the younger Churches stand still watching the population explosion? And new Churches from abroad (like the Church of God, the Church of Rome, the Adventists, and others come in to work among the neglected remainder? And non-Christian faiths like Marxism, Buddhism, Islam or Scientism multiply their followers? Will the simple device of laying a burden on a younger Church cause it to act?

Let us, second, plead the cause for World Mission assuming this responsibility. Here is a responsive population. Here are large numbers of able national Christians. What better place for world mission to invest resources so that the land will become solidly Christian? Assisted by the mission, the Church will develop a Christian frame work of society. The younger Churches say to World Mission, "We shall carry on the churches already established and help with evangelization all we can. You must pioneer. As fast as churches are estabished, turn them over to us and we shall perfect them." From many points of view this seems a sensible decision.

Yet, alas, merely turning the main task over to World Mission is no answer. What happens when World Mission, its resources already committed to many good activities, also stands by watching the population explode?

Neither in other lands nor in Jamaica will successful completion of mission depend primarily on right organizational relationships between Jerusalem and Antioch. In Jamaica what is stopped dead in its tracks is "the Church and its assisting Mission". What did not grow for over a century was precisely "a partnership in obedience".

In the following respect too, Jamaica furnishes a preview of other lands. A plateau in church growth easily occurs when stage one has been completed. Once any proportion of a population has become Christian, both Church and Mission find abundant work to do among church members. Mission becomes aid to static churches.

Perfecting the saints is emphasized. While leaders talk about "evangelism" and "bearing witness to Christ," they allow winnable multitudes to remain unwon. While they engage in many desirable activities, the growth of the churches barely keeps pace with that of the population.

This was the process by which North Africa was lost to Islam before 700 A.D. The population was composed of three strata—the Italian, the Punic, and the Berber. The Italian stratum was completely won to Christian Faith. The Punic stratum was partly won. And then the Church of North Africa, indeed the Church of the great Augustine, found abundant work to do with existing Christians. It did not press on to convert the Berber multitudes. They were enormously winnable; but the Church did not win them. It made no effort to disciple the Berber masses *at their level*. Becoming a Christian meant becoming a part of cultured Italo-Punic society. The illiterate barbarous peasants were stopped from becoming Christians not by religious considerations so much as by cultural ones. When Islam defeated the armies of Rome, while she did not force Christians to become Moslems, she gave the pagan masses (as she had the pagan Arabs) the option of Islam or war. Almost overnight North Africa became an Islamic country.

The main stage of mission must be tackled with the kind of a younger Church depicted in the preceding chapter. The difficulties to be surmounted are those inherent in these congregations—not congregations in England or America. The ways of surmounting them will be ways possible to these congregations.

One asks, "In the light of this specific population, these specific problems, and this kind of churches, what

must World Mission (including the Churches in Jamaica)
now do to lead the unchurched to rest their faith intelli-
gently on Christ? How do we finish the main stage of
mission?

II. **The Indefinitely Reproduceable Pattern**.

The present pattern of church cannot be spread much
further. It has multiplied about as much as it can. This
upper class kind of church cannot be extended into the
masses without large subsidies. Buildings, ministers,
travel, overhead—all cost too much for working class
people to pay. A simpler kind of church, more indigenous
to mass life is required.

Mission must develop a pattern of church which is
indefinitely reproduceable *among the masses by the masses,
and at their level.* It cannot wait to lift the masses to the
level of the upper class churches. To wait would be wrong
in the sight of God in that it would condemn millions to
live and die without becoming disciples of Christ merely
because they are poor. To wait would be imprudent too,
in that it would expose the masses to the temptations of
magic and animism, and the blandishments of pseudo-
absolutes and man-made religions.

Churches of the masses—self-supporting, self-direct-
ing and self propagating—are urgently needed. The new
masses will not come into feudal Churches today. The
pattern by which Scotch peasants became Christian and
were happy to have their lords and ministers live on a
much higher scale and manage the Church is increasingly
less possible today. Common men of today will unite with
the church at their own level and according to their own
sociological structures. They will not flock to churches

in which they are always appendages to the classes. They want churches in which they feel at home, in whose direction they play the chief part, and whose ministry—made up of their own men—they can support at the level of their own incomes.

To be sure the Church should unite a population, not divide it into classes; and elevate it, not lead it to contentment at its own level. Yet Christ and the Church can unite and elevate only populations which come into the Church. Until the tribes come in as tribes, they cannot be unified into nations. The process of unification is nothing which happens overnight; but in the Church it does happen—and fairly rapidly too.

In creating the indefinitely reproduceable pattern we must make a clear distinction between cultural improvement and salvation. Theology and the Bible both require this. The New Testament churches in the rabbit warrens which were ancient Jerusalem and in what the western world today would call "the squalid little villages on the Judean hills" met in homes for years before building churches. When they built, the structures were in keeping with their economic ability. What the Church confers is reconciliation to God at the level of culture, education, and possessions which a given population enjoys.

How shall we get churches of the masses which are also soundly Christian? Here the cultural overhang of the western trained churchmen can play a most damaging part. It is so easy for him to think that being "soundly Christian" involves the degree of wealth, training, education, and leisure to which he is accustomed. One reason why the Pentecostal churches have multiplied so greatly in Latin America is that they have followed a very simple pattern. For it they have been ridiculed by some western led Churches. Their demise has been expected decade by decade; but instead of dying they have multiplied exceedingly. It can be taken as axiomatic that any kind of church simple enough to spread naturally in the masses will appear "scarcely Christian" to the privileged of the earth (Eastern as well as Western). The churches of God in Jamaica, for example, look like a poor show compared with the fine buildings and highly educated ministers of the older denominations.

An ignorant Christianity is clearly not desirable; but then neither is a Christianity so learned as to be unable to reproduce itself in the masses. No easy solution to the dilemma exists; but we believe one can be found. Our Lord wants Galilean peasants and fishermen discipled. The life of neither men nor churches consists in the abundance of their possessions.

A hopeful aspect of the situation is "the tide." A drive for abundant life marks the nations today. The common man will certainly rise. Malaria will certainly be banished. Illiteracy will disappear. The income of the masses will increase. Tomorrow they will eat much better than they do today. Enormous new releases of physical power and knowledge make such results probable. The "have" nations will help "have not" nations to a degree which would have been thought incredible a few years ago. The tide is coming in.

Churches may properly work in the direction of the tide; but their main task is not to lift a few ignorant poor into the exploiting upper classes. It is to bring multitudes to Christ at the level where they are, that believing on Him they may find eternal—and abundant—life. In so doing

Churches will also bring much more social and economic advances than they could by direct action.

Mergers among middle and upper class Churches have certain values. Church union produces a stronger Church. Yet the gulfs to be bridged are not only those of polity and doctrine but the massive differences in income, education, and opportunity which separate the churched from the unchurched and the Churches of the masses from the Churches of the classes. More potent than ecclesiastical pride as a source of division is class-pride and wealth-pride. Churchmen, who think solely in terms of the theological and ritual causes of divisions in England and America, miss the real issues in Jamaica—and some other lands. Ecumenicity between the Churches of the controlling classes and those of the oppressed masses is needed— an ecumenicity which assumes that less privileged Churches are just as valid as more privileged.

III. **Eliminating the Dark River**.

The Church in Jamaica convinced that Pattern II is displeasing to God, should liberate those in bondage to it. Decade after decade to live reluctantly with a custom which bars such a high per cent of the population so effectively from the Church is intolerable and unnecessary.

The present policy of the Church has reached an impasse. It continues a state of affairs where ninety per cent of the 15-35 year age group is barred from the Church. No amount of success in the classes and in rescuing couples in later life from the Dark River can compensate for the loss of hundreds of thousands during these vital years.

The present policy of the Church admits to full membership only those who intend to live by Christian sexual

standards.   This is good as far as it goes.   To it should be
added a direct attack on the institution of concubinage.
Churches should campaign actively for the kind of economy, laboring conditions, remuneration, and housing
which permit and encourage Christian sex mores.

The Churches can combine social action, Christian
education, remedial legislation, early marriage, and sound
conversion in a united drive against this evil. Until the
Dark River as a recognized part of the country's drainage
system is dried up, neither a pattern for the masses nor
anything else is likely to secure much church growth.

The Dark River is not merely a Jamaican stream.
It is a symbol of customs which throughout the world keep
men and women from becoming disciples. Often the
Church is powerless to change these customs. Then it
can make disciples of only those who break with the custom, hoping that as disciples increase, the custom will
be weakened. But now and again God gives His Church
power to break the custom itself. In the 19th Century
the Church excised the institution of slavery—long a can-
cer in the body of humanity. The curse of drink was bro-
ken in the United States around 1920 and—though Christian forces suffered a disastrous defeat on this front there-
after—for a few years thousands of communities enjoyed
real liberation. In 1922 I preached in a town where,
after prohibition came in, the jail—always full up to that
time—had no inmate for five years. In South India,
Hindu law prohibited Untouchable women from wearing
clothing above the waist, until (over a hundred years ago)
the churches campaigned against the restriction and Christian women from among the Untouchables went quietly to
jail for the sin of covering their bodies. They kept on

going to jail till the law was repealed. Wherever the Church is granted this power, God expects her to use it to make the framework of society more Christian.

In all such matters, now that the days of western empires have ended, nationals must take the initiative. The guest missionary (from Korea or Kansas) cannot lead in changing national customs. He simply helps to create a conscience sensitive to social cancers and to uphold the hands of those courageous prophets who propose to cut them out.

IV. Recapturing a Concern for the Salvation of Men.

The main meanings which world mission can discern in Jamaica remain weak and poor without this fourth. Nothing significant is likely to happen unless World Mission can amplify in existing Christians and missionaries a passion for the salvation of their neighbors. Converts are not picked up while strolling along the beach. Faith is ignited only by a blazing flame of faith. No one without the Saviour brings men to the Saviour. A consciousness of the main task of mission, an indefinitely reproduceable pattern, a resolution to dry up the Dark River—all are powerless without a genuine concern for the salvation of men.

Perhaps this passion for salvation will embody itself in revivals in the tradition of Fox, Wesley, and Moody followed by shepherding of converts on an unprecedented scale. Perhaps some Church, possessed of the Holy Spirit will manifest the shepherd heart more greatly than the others and grow enormously. Perhaps a Jamaican of mighty spiritual stature will arise who will speak to his people.

Whatever the manner of its coming, the test of its arrival will be that multitudes out of the Church are converted, come in, start to live holy lives, and multiply their churches.

World Mission, clear as to the goal, might well pour itself out in prayer toward this end. The Church of Christ (all Branches) at prayer for a new Pentecost among the unchurched myriads would release God's power. Bands of men and women all over the island praying for a new descent of the Holy Spirit might well be today, as at Antioch, a sign that the wall between the Jews and the Gentiles was being breached.

Before this can happen, we shall have to abandon the comfortable rationalizations with which we defend our ineffectiveness in persuading men to become disciples of Christ. Understandings of mission which enable the Church in Jamaica (and elsewhere) to stand still for a hundred years in the midst of a winnable and exploding population must be repented of. We shall have to measure evangelistic effectiveness by the number of the lost brought in and kept in the fold. Specially necessary is distinguishing between the start of the process and the completion, between disciplining and perfecting, between the wicket gate and the pearly portals. Perfecting is good; but it must not be allowed to displace disciplining.

Conclusion

Jamaica has much to say to Christian Mission in many lands. Despite her individual island personality, the structure of her society and Churches is startlingly like that of many other lands. The "Population versus Communicants" Graph (opposite page 19) could be dupli-

cated in many other fields. Mounting mission aid accompanied by minor church growth (graph opposite page 104) is met elsewhere. Class-mass society is characteristic of many countries of Africasia. A younger Church which started out middle class or pressed upward into the middle class is such an ordinary sight that some consider lifting a Church into the middle class the *raison d'etre* of missions! The struggle of the Church with sub-Christian sex mores is very common. Yes, Jamaica has much to say.

Yet some churchmen may rejoice rather in seeing exactly the sociological, spiritual and cultural conditions of the Jamaican Churches. In truth Christian Mission needs a deep understanding of the true state of the younger Churches. The vagueness of global generalities, the ambiguities of work carried on in hope, the fog of promotional pleading which proves "all our work worthy of support" must be swept aside by serious misologists and the younger Churches seen as they are. Then Churches will be able to chart their path better, assisting missions multiply them better, and the Holy Spirit find Christians more responsive as He leads them to disciple the nations.

Printed by Rev. W. W. Bell at the Lucknow Publishing House, Lucknow—(2000)—74—4-8-1961